User's Handbook To
IBM BASIC©

USER'S HANDBOOK TO IBM BASIC©

1st EDITION

Jeffrey Weber

Weber Systems, Inc.
Cleveland, Ohio

Published by:
Weber Systems, Inc.
8437 Mayfield Road
Cleveland, Ohio 44026

For information on translations and book distributors outside of the United States, please contact WSI at the above address.

User's Handbook To IBM BASIC©   **First Edition**

Library of Congress Catalog Card Number 82-051012
ISBN 0-938862-14-6

Typesetting: Beth Cammarn

CONTENTS

1. INTRODUCTION TO THE IBM PC   **9.**

Overview 9. System Board 12. ROM 14. RAM 15. BIOS 16. CPU 20. Intel 8088 21. Intel 8087 22. Cassette BASIC 24. Disk BASIC 24. Advanced BASIC 24. Disk Drives 25. Hard Disks 27. Winchester Disk Drives 27. Floppy Diskettes 28. Tracks & Sectors 29. Hard & Soft Sectors 30. Write Protection 32. Disk Operating Systems 33. IBM DOS 34. CP/M-86 34. UCSD p-System 35. Compiled vs. Interpreted Language 37. Monochrome Display 38. IBM CPS-80 Printer 39. Serial & Parallel Communications 41. Monochrome Display/Printer Adapter Card 42. Color Graphics Monitor Adapter 45. A/N Mode 45. APA Mode 47. Asynchronous Communications Adapter 47. IBM Keyboard 48. IBM Printer Operation 57. PC Start-Up Procedure 59. BASIC Command Entry 61.

2. INTRODUCTION TO BASIC   **63.**

Versions of IBM BASIC 63. Command & Execute Mode 64. Entering a Program 65. BASIC Constants 67. BASIC Variables 67. BASIC Variable Names 68. Integer, Single, and Double Precision Data 69.

3. BEGINNING IBM BASIC   **71.**

BASIC Statement Structure 71. Arithmetic Operators 72. Exponentiation 73. Mixing Variable Types 73. Order of Evaluation 74.

Relational Operators 76. Remark Statements 78. Outputting Data 79. Inputting Data 80. Loops 81. Conditional Statements 83. Branching Statements 83.

4. MORE IBM BASIC CONCEPTS   **87.**

Tables & Arrays 87. DATA, READ Statements 90. Subroutines & GOSUB 93. Advanced Printing 95. Formatting Characters 96. Line Width 99. Random Number Generator 100. String Handling 101. String Concatenation 101. Comparing Strings 102. String Handling Functions 103. String/Numeric Data Conversion 106. Mathematical Functions 108. User-Defined Functions 112. Graphics 112. Text Mode 113. Medium Resolution Graphics Mode 114. Logical Operators 117. Order of Evaluation 112.

5. FILES & FILE HANDLING WITH IBM BASIC   **123.**

Introduction 123. Files, Records, & Fields 123. File Specifications 125. Opening & Closing a File 126. Random & Sequential Access 129. Saving & Loading Programs in Cassette BASIC 130. Data Files on Cassette 131. IBM BASIC & Diskette Files 132. Using Floppy Diskettes 133. Storing DOS 136. Copying DOS 137. Verifying DISKCOPY 140. System Level 141. More DOS Commands 142. Changing The Current Drive 143. Saving & Loading Diskette Files 144. Data Files on Diskette 144.

6. ADVANCED CONCEPTS   **147.**

Alt Key & BASIC 147. Entering a BASIC Program 147. Editing an IBM BASIC Program 148. Errors & Debugging 154.

7. REFERENCE GUIDE   **157.**

Introduction 157. ABS 158. ASC 158. ATN 159. AUTO 159. BEEP 161. BLOAD 161. BSAVE 163.

CALL 163. CDBL 164. CHAIN 165. CHR$ 166. CINT 167. CIRCLE 167. CLEAR 168. CLOSE 169. CLS 169. COLOR 170. COM 173. COMMON 174. CONT 174. COS 175. CSNG 175. CRSLIN 176. CVI, CVS, CVD 176. DATA 177. DATE$ 177. DEF FN 179. DEFDBL 180. DEFSTR 180. DEFINT 180. DEFSNG 180. DEF SEG 181. DEF USR 182. DELETE 182. DIM 183. DRAW 183. EDIT 185. END 186. EOF 186. ERASE 187. ERR,ERL 188. ERROR 189. EXP 190. FIELD 190. FILES 191. FIX 192. FOR...NEXT 193. FRE 195. GET 196. GOSUB, RETURN 198. GOTO 199. HEX$ 199. IF 200. INKEY$ 201. INP 202. INPUT 204. INPUT# 204. INPUT$ 205. INSTR 206. INT 207. KEY 208. KILL 210. LEFT$ 211. LEN 211. LET 212. LINE 212. LINE INPUT 214. LINE INPUT# 215. LIST 216. LLIST 217. LOAD 218. LOC 219. LOCATE 220. LOF 221. LOG 222. LPOS 223. LPRINT 223. LPRINT USING 224. LSET, RSET 225. MERGE 226. MID$ 227. MKI$, MKS$, MKD$ 228. MOTOR 229. NAME 230. NEW 230. OCT$ 231. ON COM 231. ON ERROR 233. ON...GOSUB, ON...GOTO 234. ON KEY 235. ON PEN 236. ON STRIG 237. OPEN 238. OPEN COM 240. OPTION BASE 242. OUT 242. PAINT 243. PEEK 244. PEN 245. PLAY 246. POINT 248. POKE 249. POS 250. PRINT 250. PRINT USING 251. PRINT#, PRINT USING# 255. PSET, PRESET 257. PUT 258. RANDOMIZE 261. READ 261. REM 262. RENUM 263. RESET 264. RESTORE 264. RESUME 265. RETURN 266. RIGHT$ 267. RND 268. RUN 269. SAVE 270. SCREEN 271. SGN 273. SIN 273. SOUND 274. SPACE$ 275. STR$ 278. STRIG 279. STRING$ 280. SWAP 281. SYSTEM 282. TAB 282. TAN 283. TIME$ 283. TRON, TROFF 284. USR 285. VAL 286. VARPTR 287. WAIT 287. WHILE, WEND 288. WIDTH 289. WRITE 290. WRITE# 291.

Appendix A. BASIC Reserved Words   293.

Appendix B. IBM PC Device Names   294.

Appendix C. IBM BASIC Error Messages   295.

Appendix D. ASCII Character Codes   300.

Appendix E. Extended Codes For INKEY$ 303.

Index   303.

CHAPTER 1.
INTRODUCTION TO THE IBM PC

Overview

The introduction of the Personal Computer by IBM caused a revolution in the microcomputer industry. The IBM Personal Computer is called by many the best microcomputer yet brought to market.

In an industry previously dominated by Apple computer, Commodore International, and Tandy, IBM is creating a competitive stir. IBM microcomputer sales are estimated to grow from $360 million in 1982 to $2.3 billion by 1986. The retail value of IBM software sold is estimated to grow from $85 million in 1982 to $700 million by 1986. The value of PC hardware related items made by other companies is estimated to grow from $65 million in 1982 to $685 million by 1986. The value of software related sales made by other firms is estimated to grow from $15 million in 1982 to $395 million by 1986.

The total for all of the above categories should exceed $4 billion by 1986. In short, IBM will create a $4 billion industry with its Personal Computer.

The basic IBM Personal Computer consists of two separate units; the **Keyboard** and the **System Unit.** These are shown in Illustration 1-1.

The Keyboard Unit consists of a main keyboard with a standard typewriter style keyboard layout. To the left of the main keyboard is a numeric keypad. To the right of the main keyboard is a set of 10 function keys. A total of 83 keys are contained on the keyboard unit.

The keyboard unit is connected to the System Unit via a coiled cable. The System Unit contains the heart of the PC--an Intel 8088 microprocessor, up to 64K of **dynamic RAM** (Random Access Memory), the 40K extended Microsoft BASIC in **ROM**

(Read-Only Memory), up to to two disk drives, a cassette interface, a built-in speaker, and five expansion slots. Additional **dynamic** RAM memory cards can be placed into the expansion slots to bring the total amount of RAM to 256K.

Additional peripherals can be purchased to round out your basic IBM PC into a total microcomputer system. These include the IBM Monochrome Display, which is the video display terminal for the system, and the IBM 80 CPS Matrix Printer. (The 80 CPS stands for 80 characters per second--the printer's speed.) These items are pictured in Illustration 1-1.

Illustration 1-1. IBM PC System Unit & Keyboard

Table 1-1. IBM PC System Components

Component	Description
System Unit — Size:	Width 20 inches, depth 16 inches, height 5.5 inches; weight (without drives) 21 pounds, weight (with 2 disk drives) 28 pounds.
Power:	120 VAC
Processor:	Intel 8088
Standard Features:	Keyboard Unit & Cable Cassette Recorder Connector; Five Expansion Slots; BASIC interpreter; 16K RAM.
Disk Drives	Up to two 5 inch Floppy Disk Drives. 160K each.
Operating System	IBM PC DOS (Microsoft)
Optional Hardware	Monochrome Video Display
	Combination Monochrome Display Adapter and Printer Adapter.
	Color Graphics Monitor Adapter
	16K RAM expansion
	32K RAM expansion
	64K RAM expansion
	Disk Drive Adapter
	Disk Drive (5 inch Floppy Disks)
	Asynchronous Communications Adapter

Table 1-1. IBM PC System Components (Cont.)

Component	Description
	Game Control Adapter
	Printer
	Printer Adapter
	Printer Cable
	Printer Stand
Available Software (2/1/82)	BASIC Interpreter (Microsoft) standard.
	Extended BASIC Interpreter (Microsoft)
	PASCAL Compiler (Microsoft)
	Visicalc (Personal Software)
	Peachtree Accounting System
	Adventure (Microsoft)
	Advanced Diagnostics Package

System Board

The System Board, or motherboard, is the main circuit board of a microcomputer system. Most of the circuitry for the PC is placed on its System Board including:

Microprocessor(s)	Expansion Slots
ROM Memory	Cassette Interface
RAM Memory	Keyboard Interface
DMA Circuits	Speaker and Timing Circuits

Illustration 1-2. IBM System Board

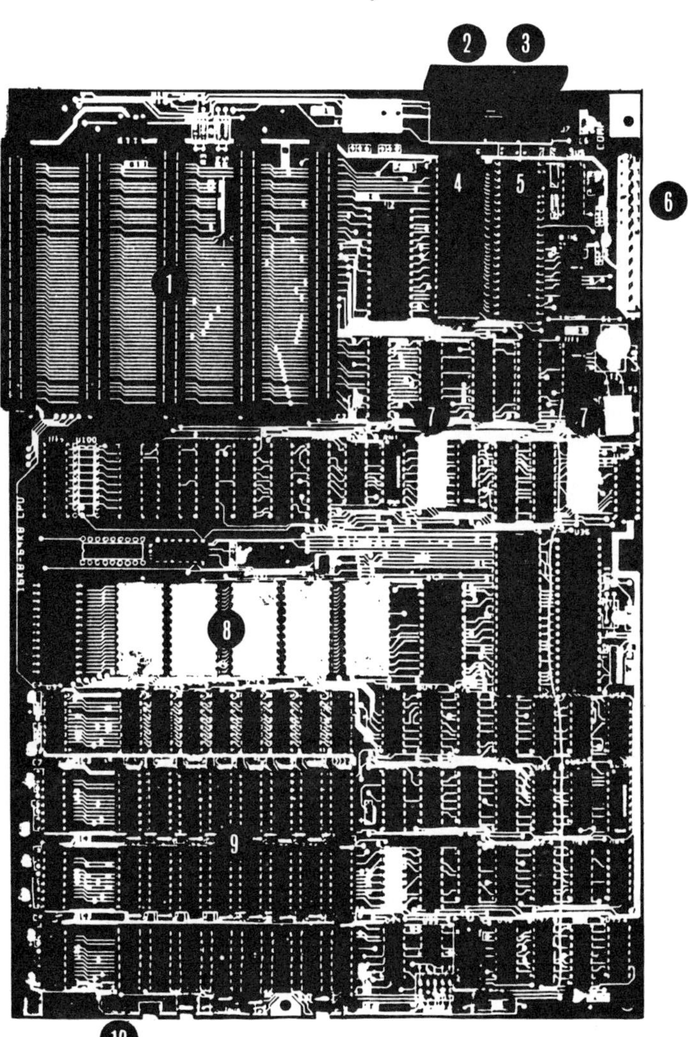

1 -- Expansion slots	6 -- Power supply connection
2 -- Cassette connection	7 -- DIP switches
3 -- Keyboard unit connection	8 -- ROM chips
4 -- Intel 8088 CPU	9 -- RAM chips
5 -- 8087 co-processor socket	10 -- Speaker connection

ROM And RAM

ROM stands for Read-Only Memory. ROM will hold the data stored in it permanently. If the power to the PC is shut off, the information stored in ROM will remain there. As previously mentioned, the Microsoft BASIC language interpreter is stored in ROM.

RAM stands for Random Access Memory.* Any data stored in RAM is lost when the PC's power is shut off. When data is loaded from a tape cassette, a disk drive, or the keyboard, it is stored in RAM.

Dynamic And Static RAM

There are two different types of RAM memory; **dynamic RAM** and **static RAM.** Dynamic RAM can only hold the data it is storing for a few milliseconds. Therefore, any data being stored in dynamic RAM must constantly be rewritten or refreshed. This dynamic RAM refresh function must be a part of the support logic when the dynamic RAM memory is designed.

Static RAM is more expensive than dynamic RAM. However, once data has been written into static RAM, it will be retained as long as power is supplied. A description of the ROM and RAM used in the IBM PC is given in Tables 1-2 and 1-3 respectively.

IBM ROM

As mentioned in the previous section, ROM is a type of memory that will hold the data stored in it permanently. The IBM PC uses ROM to store programs that are essential to the operation of the computer.

These programs being stored in ROM are often called **firmware** (software in hardware). The IBM PC uses ROM to store its **BIOS, BASIC interpreter,** and **bootstrap loader.**

---

* Random Access Memory is a somewhat misleading term to describe RAM, as most memory (including ROM) is randomly accessed.

The bootstrap loader is a start-up program that starts the disk drive and then loads the computer's operating system from the system diskette.

The IBM PC's ROM is contained on the System Board. Although, the System Board has the capability of holding six 8K ROM chips, only five of the six sockets are currently utilized. IBM may be planning to use the sixth socket for a future enhancement to the PC.

In addition to the 64K of ROM possible on the System Board, an additional 192K is available for use by placing ROM expansion cards in the expansion slots. This additional ROM capacity might be used at some future date for placing applications software on ROM or including additional BIOS routines for adding new peripherals to the PC.

Table 1-2. IBM ROM (Read-Only Memory)

IBM ROM Capacity	
Manufacturer:	Motorola
Total Capacity:	256K (48K Capacity on System Board)
Currently Used:	40K on System Board; 5-8K ROM's
Programs in ROM:	BIOS, BASIC Interpreter

IBM RAM

As previously mentioned, RAM is a type of memory meant for temporary storage of data.

The IBM PC comes equipped with 16K of RAM on its System Board. An additional 48K of RAM may be added to the System Board. The first 16K of RAM is wired into place on the System Board, while the additional 48K are placed in sockets, so as to allow non-technicians to easily expand the computer's RAM capacity.

Each 16K of RAM on the System Board consists of 9 chips, each with a 2K capacity. On the surface, it appears as if this is one chip too many.

However, the IBM PC uses the ninth memory chip to perform **parity checks** on the other RAM chips. Parity checks are constant tests conducted on the RAM in which the number of individual bits which are "on" is added and rechecked to be certain that no data has been lost. If the RAM should fail a parity check test, the following message will appear on the screen,

PARITY ERROR

and the program currently being run will be aborted.

In addition to the System Board's 64K RAM capacity, an additional 192K of RAM can be added to the PC by adding RAM expansion cards into the expansion slots inside the PC System Unit. IBM distributes 32K and 64K RAM expansion cards for this purpose.

The PC's 8088 microprocessor allows up to 1 **megabyte** (one million bytes) of addressable memory. Of that 1 megabyte, 128K is utilized by the PC for the Graphics and Display Adapter, 256K is utilized for ROM, and 640K are utilized for RAM. Therefore, space exists for an additional 384K of RAM. This may be a future development on the part of IBM.

IBM BIOS

BIOS is an abbreviation for the term BASIC Input/Output System. The BIOS is a collection of programs that control the transfer of characters between the microprocessor and the various devices connected to it (i.e. printer, video display, keyboard, communications adapter, etc.).

The PC's BIOS also contains the cassette tape operating system, a power-up self-test, the graphics character generator, the

Table 1-3. IBM RAM (Random Access Memory)

IBM RAM Capacity	
RAM Type:	4116 type; 2K each 250 nanosecond access time, 450 nanosecond cycle time.
Row Configuration:	16K per row; 9 chips per row (9th chip used for parity checking)
Board Configuration:	System Board--4 rows (1 row soldered, remainder placed in sockets) 32K Expansion Board 2 rows 64K Expansion Board 4 rows
RAM Capacity:	System Board--16K (standard) System Board--48K (possible expansion) Expansion Slots--192K (additional) Possible Future Expansion- 384K
RAM Characteristics:	Dynamic RAM usable with Direct Memory Addressing (DMA)

System Configuration analysis program (which gives the memory size and peripherals used), a time of day clock, and a mini-floppy disk drive bootstrap loader.

Microcomputers designed around 8-bit microprocessors tend to limit the number and size of programs stored in BIOS because the 8-bit microprocessor can address only a fraction of the memory that a 16-bit processor can. The PC with its 16-bit microprocessor and its ability to address up to 1 MB allows for the more extensive use of ROM.

One advantage to placing the BIOS in ROM is that its programs are available when the computer is turned on. However, placing BIOS in ROM also presents some difficulties, in that the BIOS routines may not be changed to allow for the addition of new devices.

IBM has provided for the addition of devices to its ROM based BIOS, without actually changing the ROM chips, by reserving several Interrupt Vectors. Even so, it may eventually be necessary to replace the ROM chips currently used in the PC's System Board, if the BIOS is to be changed substantially.

Table 1-4. IBM BIOS (BASIC Input/Output System) Features

IBM BIOS
Purpose: BIOS controls the transfer of data between the microprocessor and various system devices (i.e. keyboard, video display, printer, communications card, etc.).
Designed By: Microsoft, Inc.
Location: 8K ROM Chip contained on System Board.
Programs: 1. Cassette Operating System 2. Power-On Self-Test 3. I/O routines for video display, keyboard, printer, and communications adapter 4. Graphics Character Generator 5. System Configuration Analysis (memory size, peripherals used) 6. Time-of-Day Clock 7. Mini-Floppy Disk Drive Bootstrap Loader

Table 1-5. IBM BIOS Interrupt Vectors

Interrupt Number		Name	BIOS Initialization
0		Divide by Zero	None
1		Single Step	None
2		Non Maskable	NMI_INT (F000:E2C3)
3		Breakpoint	None
4		Overflow	None
5		Print Screen	PRINT_SCREEN (F000:FF54)
6		Unused	
7		Unused	
8		Time of Day	TIMER_INT(F000:FEA5)
9		Keyboard	KB_INT (F000:E987)
A		Unused	
B	8259	Unused	
C	Interrupt Vectors	Unused (Reserved Communications)	
D		Unused	
E		Diskette	DISK_INT (F000:EF57)
F		Unused (Reserved Printer)	
10		Video	VIDEO_I O (F000:F065)
11		Equipment Check	EQUIPMENT (F000:F84D)
12		Memory	MEMORY_SIZE_DETERMINE (F000:F8411)
13		Diskette	DISKETTE_I O (F000:EC59)
14	BIOS	Communications	RS232_I O (F000:E739)
15	Entry	Cassette	CASSETTE_I O (F000:F859)
16	Points	Keyboard	KEYBOARD_ I O (F000:E82E)
17		Printer	PRINTER_I O (F000:EF02)
18		Cassette BASIC	(F600:0000)
19		Bootstrap	BOOT_STRAP (F000:E6F2)
1A		Time of Day	TIME_OF_DAY (F000:FEGE)
1B		Keyboard Break	DUMMY_RETURN (F000:FF53)
1C		Timer Tick	DUMMY_RETURN (F000:FF53)
1D		Video Initialization	VIDEO_PARMS (F000:F0A4)
1E		Diskette Parameters	DISK_BASE (F000:EFC7)
1F		Video Graphics Chars	None

IBM's CPU

The central processing unit or **CPU** is the heart of any computer. The CPU controls all of the other components for the computer.

In larger computers, the CPU and the **ALU** (Arithmetic Logic Unit), consist of a group of IC chips each dedicated to its own task. In smaller computers, the CPU and ALU are generally combined on a single chip, which is known as a **microprocessor**.

A microprocessor can be defined as a single chip which contains the logic of a central processing unit as well as any additional logic that must complement the CPU.

The microprocessor used in the PC is the Intel 8088, which is manufactured by Intel Corporation of Sunnyvale, California. Intel is a pioneer in the development of microprocessors. Intel developed the predecessor of the 8088, the 4004 calculator chip, in the early 1970's. Subsequently, the 8008, 8080, 8085, and 8088/8086 microprocessors were developed. The difference between the 8088 and 8086 will be discussed shortly.

Microprocessor logic is based upon the **bit.** A bit is the basis of all information storage within the computer. A bit consists of a simple switch which can consist of either of the two binary states, on or off.

Bits are often separated into groups of eight. These groups of 8 bits are known as a **byte**. A byte is required to represent a single character (i.e. letter, number, or symbol). Generally, bytes are processed by the computer in groups of 2.

Most of the 8-bit microprocessors can only **address** (or work directly with) 65,535 (64K) bytes at any one time. Even though this number appears large, a 30 page document would fill this memory area.

Most 16-bit microprocessors can address from 256,000 to 16 million bytes of memory. Moreover, 16-bit microprocessors process data at a speed from 2 to 10 times faster than 8-bit microprocessors.

Illustration 1-3. Close-Up Of Intel 8088 Chip

Intel 8088 CPU

One of the main advantages which the IBM PC has over other microcomputers is the power provided by its use of the 8088 CPU.

The 8088 can address up to one million bytes of memory (or 1 megabyte, abbreviated as 1MB). The 8088 has 20 different address lines, which allows 2 to exponent 20 (2^{20}) different address combinations. This is the equivalent of 1,048,576 different addresses.

The speed of the 8088 is approximately .65 mps (or million operations per second). In other words, the 8088 will process 650,000 arithmetic operations or data transfers per second. When compared with the Intel 8080A, the 8088 is approximately six times faster.

The characteristics of the 8088 are outlined in Table 1-6.

Table 1-6. Intel 8088 Characteristics

Intel 8088	
Construction:	Chip technology--HMOS 40 pin plastic package
Manufacturer:	Intel Corporation
Introduction Date:	1979
Features:	1. 20 address line
	2. 1MB memory addressing
	3. 650,000 operations per second
	4. 8 data lines
	5. 4.77 MhZ clock speed
	6. Separate bus interface and execution units
	7. 99 basic machine languages instructions
	8. Software compatible with Intel 8086

Intel 8087 Numeric Data Processor

Most CPU's perform mathematic operations relatively slowly--especially when non-integer numbers are involved. This is due to the fact that on non-integer numbers, the microprocessor must be given instructions on how to perform math calculations.

To speed the processing of math operations, many mini- and

main-frame computers use a separate processor to perform numeric operations. These are known as math processors or floating point co-processors.

A math processor contains the internal logic needed to perform math operations internally, rather than relying on an external set of program constructions. Math processors can outperform CPU's by a factor of as much as 100 to 1.

The Intel 8087 Numeric Data Processor is the math co-processor for the Intel 8086 and 8088 CPU's. Full-scale production of the 8087 is expected in the middle of 1982.

The System Board for the IBM PC contains a 40-pin socket which is named the Aux Processor Socket. The circuit lines running to this empty socket are for the eventual addition of the Intel 8087 math co-processor.

Table 1-7. Intel 8087 Characteristics

Intel 8087 Numeric Data Processor
Manufacturer: Intel Corporation
Introduction Date: 1980
Characteristics: 1. Includes built-in math instructions for addition, subtraction, multiplication, division, square root, absolute value, tangent, arctangent, and others 2. Handles integers up to 18 digits in length and floating point numbers 16 to 80 bits wide. 3. Compatible with Intel 8086/8088 microprocessors.

It is expected that when the 8087 is available for use with the IBM PC, the PC will experience an increase in numeric processing speed by a factor of at least 20.

The characteristics of the Intel 8087 are given in Table 1-7.

Microsoft BASIC Interpreter

Microsoft BASIC is the version of BASIC that is standard with the IBM PC. The BASIC **interpreter** (explained on page 37) is contained in 40K of ROM. The various features of Microsoft BASIC will be discussed in detail throughout the remainder of this book. Our discussion here is merely meant to be an introduction.

The IBM PC uses three separate versions of BASIC; Cassette BASIC, Disk BASIC, and Advanced BASIC.

Cassette BASIC is the version of BASIC used when a cassette recorder is being used to store information. Cassette BASIC can not be used when data is being stored on diskettes.

Disk BASIC contains all of the capabilities of Cassette BASIC and can also be used when data is being stored on diskettes. In other words, Disk BASIC can be used when data is being stored on diskettes or when it is being stored on cassette tape.

Advanced BASIC has all of the capabilities of Cassette BASIC and Disk BASIC as well as additional features not found on these other two versions of BASIC. Advanced BASIC includes several graphics commands such as CIRCLE, DRAW, and PAINT which allow the user to fully utilize the graphics capabilities of the IBM PC when it is equipped with the Color/Graphics Monitor Adapter and a color monitor or color television set.

Both the Advanced BASIC and the Disk BASIC versions require DOS before they can be run, or before any programs written in Advanced or Disk BASIC can be run. DOS is required to manage the input and output from your disk units.

IBM PC Peripherals

In the remaining sections of Chapter 1, we will discuss some of
the peripheral components that can be added to your IBM PC.
These include the following:

> Disk Drives
> Monochrome Display
> IBM 80 CPS Printer
> Monochrome Display/Printer Adapter Card
> Color/Graphics Monitor Adapter Card
> Color Monitors
> Asynchronous Communications Adapter

Disk Drives And DOS

The optional disk drives for the IBM PC are **soft sectored, double
density,** and **single sided** drives. The floppy disk drives use 40
tracks per disk with eight 512 byte **sectors** per track. This gives a
total of 163,840 bytes of data storage per drive.

The IBM Disk Operating System (DOS) is a group of programs
which allow the user to manipulate information between the
diskette drives, memory, and the video screen.

Disk Drives Explained

The disk drive is one of the most important parts of a computer
system. Disk drives allow the storage of large amounts of storage.
An IBM 5¼ inch disk can store 163,840 characters of data. This is
approximately three and one half times as much data as can be
stored on 48K of RAM.

Unlike RAM storage, when information is stored on a disk, the
information is not lost when the computer is turned off. In other
words, disks offer a permanent means of storing data.

A disk stores data in a magnetic form, much like data is stored on
magnetic tape. The main difference between storage on a
magnetic tape and storage on a disk is that the disk surface is
round--much like a record's surface.

The disk drive contains a device known as a **head**, which is used to read and write information. The computer can move the head to any position desired on the disk surface. This is in contrast to magnetic tape, where data is read from or written onto the tape in consecutive order.

This capacity to read or write data at a particular position is known as **random access**. Disk drives are known as random access storage devices. On the other hand, in cases where data must be read or written in a consecutive order, the accessing is known as **sequential access**. A cassette tape recorder is known as a sequential access device.

Table 1-8. IBM Disk Drives

IBM Disk Drives	
Purpose:	Provides storage for program and data files.
Manufacturer:	Tandon Magnetics, Inc.
Capacity:	Single-sided/double density (SSDD); rated for quad density.
	Unformatted--250K currently; potential of 500K. Formatted--160K (when using PC DOS).
	48 tracks per inch--40 tracks used; 8 sectors per track; 512 bytes per sector.
Speed:	8 ms. seek time (track to track); 25ms head setting time; 500 ms. maximum start/stop time.
	250,000 bits/second transfer rate.

Types Of Disks

There are three primary types of disks used by microcomputers; **hard disks, Winchester disks,** and **floppy diskettes.** These will be described in the following sections.

Currently, IBM offers floppy diskette storage for the IBM Personal Computer. However, it is expected that IBM will also offer Winchester disk storage in the near future.

Hard Disks

Microcomputer hard disk systems generally allow storage of 5 to 30 megabytes of data. One megabyte is the equivalent of one million bytes. The hard disk itself is made of a rigid material with a magnetic coating. The disk drive and the hard disk are separate units. The operator can remove one hard disk and replace it with another.

Winchester Disk Drives

Winchester disk drives are designed so that from 6 to 10 times more data can be stored on their surface than on a standard floppy diskette. Winchester disks must be kept very clean and

Illustration 1-4. Winchester Disk System

are extremely vulnerable to dust, dirt, and smoke.

Since they must be kept so clean, Winchester disks must be sealed inside of the disk drive. This means that Winchester disks cannot be changed.

Since Winchester disks cannot be removed, floppy disk systems often are used in conjunction with Winchester disks to allow for back-up storage. Winchester disk systems are generally used with microcomputers rather than hard disk systems. A Winchester drive is shown in Illustration 1-4.

Floppy Diskettes

The most widely used type of disk storage with microcomputers is floppy disk storage. A floppy diskette consists of a round vinyl disk which is enclosed within a plastic cover. The diskette is generally stored in a paper diskette envelope.

The plastic cover protects the diskette from damage while it is being handled by the operator. The diskette should never be removed from its plastic cover. A 5¼ inch diskette with its protective envelope is shown in Illustration 1-5.

Illustration 1-5. Mini-Floppy Diskette

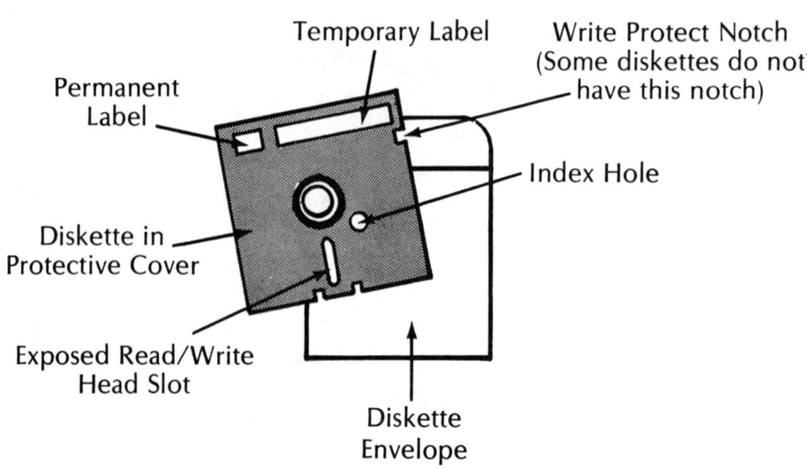

The diskette is allowed to rotate within the protective envelope. The round hole in the middle of the diskette allows the disk drive to hold the diskette and spin it. The oblong shaped opening on the protective envelope provides an area where the head can read from or write to the diskette surface.

Floppy diskettes come in two sizes: 8 inch and 5¼ inch. The 5¼ inch diskettes are also known as mini-floppy diskettes. The IBM Personal Computer uses mini-floppy diskettes.

Tracks And Sectors

To facilitate the process of searching for data on the diskette surface, that surface is divided into tracks and sectors.

Tracks may be visualized as a series of concentric circles on the diskette surface, as shown in Illustration 1-6. IBM's DOS divides a diskette into 40 tracks.

To further reduce the time necessary to search for a particular data item, IBM's DOS divides each track into 8 sectors, which are also shown in Illustration 1-6.

Illustration 1-6. Tracks And Sectors

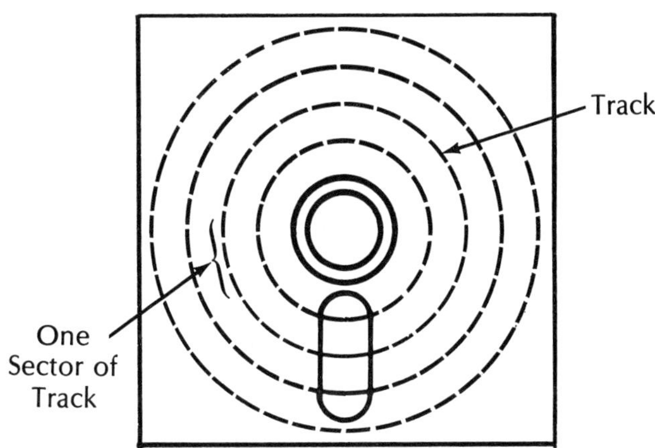

Each individual sector holds 512 bytes of data. When DOS has access to the track and sector where a particular data item is being stored, it will only have to search 512 bytes to find that item. The result of dividing the diskette surface into tracks and sectors is that access time is greatly decreased.

Hard And Soft Sectors

Locating a particular track on the disk surface is a relatively uncomplicated matter. The drive merely moves the head to the position on the diskette where the specified track is located, much like the needle on a phonograph is positioned to the location of a specific song on a record album.

However, locating a particular sector is a more difficult process. Two different methods are used to locate sectors on a disk; hard sectoring and soft sectoring.

Both the hard and soft sector methods involve the use of an index hole. The index hole is shown in Illustration 1-5. It is located just to the right of the large hole in the middle of the 5¼ inch diskette.

The index hole as shown in Illustration 1-5 is a hole only in the diskette's protective covering. Another index hole is located on the actual diskette surface inside of the envelope. As the diskette spins, the index hole (or holes) on the diskette surface passes underneath the hole in the protective envelope.

A light source inside of the disk drive shines light onto the area of the diskette containing the index hole. When an index hole on the disk surface is aligned with the index hole on the protective envelope, the light will shine through to a sensor. The sensor will relay information on the location of the index holes, which can be used to calculate the various sector locations.

Now that we have discussed the concepts of locating sectors, we will discuss the differences between hard and soft sectored diskettes. A hard sectored diskette contains a number of holes, each of which indicates the location of a sector. An extra hole is used to indicate the location of the first sector. The location of the various sectors is determined by counting the number of holes occuring after the first sector. A hard sectored diskette is depicted in Illustration 1-7.

Soft sectored diskettes have only one index hole as shown in Illustration 1-8. This solitary index hole marks the location of the first sector. By timing the rotation speed of the floppy diskette, the location of the other sectors can be determined. The IBM PC uses soft-sectored diskettes.

Illustration 1-7. Hard Sectored Diskette

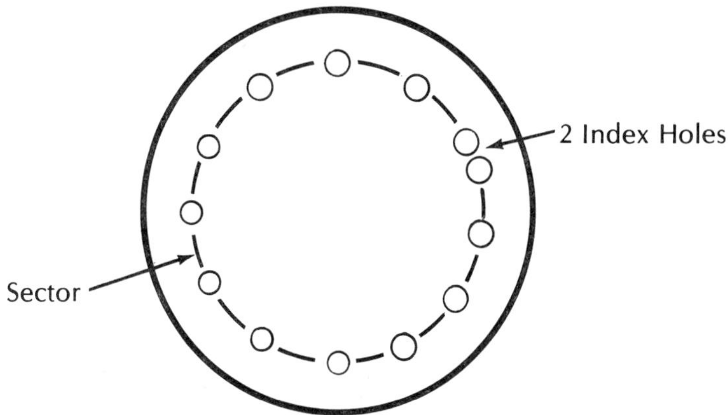

Illustration 1-8. Soft Sectored Diskette

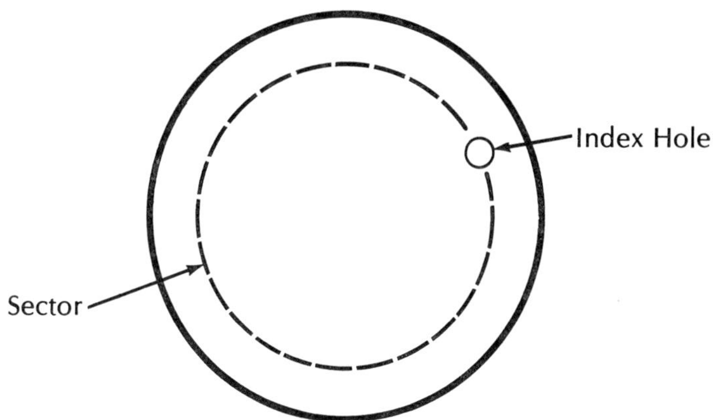

Single And Double Sided Diskettes

Some floppy diskettes are designed to be written on only one side. These are known as single sided (SS) diskettes.

Diskettes which are designed to be written on both sides are known as double sided (DS) diskettes.

Single, Double, And Quad Density Diskettes

Density refers to a diskette's recording format, which in turn affects its capacity. Single density 5¼ inch diskettes have roughly 94K of capacity, double density 5¼ inch diskettes have a capacity of about 140 to 160K, and quad density 5¼ inch diskettes have a capacity of up to 370K.

The disk drives on the IBM PC use single sided double density diskettes, although they are rated for quad density. IBM's DOS currently limits each diskette's capacity to 160K.

Diskette Write Protection

Diskettes have a notch on the side of their protective envelope which determines whether or not data can be written onto that diskette. On eight inch diskettes, this notch is known as a write-protect notch, while on 5¼ inch diskettes, it is known as a write-enable notch.

On an eight inch diskette, information cannot be written onto the diskette unless this notch has been covered. On 5¼ inch diskettes, information cannot be written onto the diskette unless the notch is left uncovered.

Some 5¼ inch diskettes (especially system diskettes) may be permanently write protected if their protective envelope does not contain a notch. Any 5¼ inch diskette with a notch can be write protected by merely covering the notch with a piece of tape as shown in Illustration 1-9.

Illustration 1-9. Write-Protecting a 5¼ Inch Diskette

Disk Operating Systems

The IBM offers not just one but three different **operating systems,** PC DOS, UCSD p-System, and CP/M 86. Each of these three operating systems undertake similar functions. However, the manner in which these functions are attained are quite different. The differences between these operating systems are very significant, and each in effect gives the PC a different personality.

An operating system can be defined as a group of programs which manage the computer's operation. A disk operating system can be defined as a group of programs that manage the transfer of data to and from a storage device such as disk or magnetic tape.

We will briefly discuss each of the currently available operating systems for the PC in the next three sections.

IBM DOS

IBM's DOS was written by Seattle Computer Products in 1980. Later, Microsoft, Inc. acquired the exclusive marketing rights to this system. Microsoft then renamed the system as MS DOS. Subsequently, Lifeboat Associates began distributing the MS DOS system under the name SB-86. IBM uses the MS DOS system under the name PC DOS.

PC DOS, MS DOS, and SB-86 are the same disk operating systems. For our purposes, we will refer to this system as PC DOS.

In some ways, DOS resembles CP/M, a disk operating system marketed by Digital Research. For example, IBM's DOS uses the same system prompt (A>) as does CP/M.

However, in actuality, IBM DOS is a version of Microsoft's Xenix operating system. Xenix is, in turn, a version of the Unix operating system which was originally developed by Western Electric.

CP/M-86

Digital Research's CP/M with over 400,000 registered users is the most widely used operating system for 8-bit microcomputers. Whether or not CP/M-86 will be maintained as a standard for 16-bit microcomputers remains to be seen.

CP/M-80 (8-bit version) is currently available on Zenith, Intertec, DEC, Wang, Xerox, and Lanier microcomputers as well as selected microcomputers manufactured by the industry leaders, Apple and Tandy.

CP/M was developed by Dr. Gary Kildall while he was an engineer at Intel Corporation. Intel had recently developed the 8008 microprocessor. Dr. Kildall and his associates had written a high level compiler known as PL/M to work with the chip. To help with the development of PL/M, the initial version of CP/M was developed in its primitive form, CP/M was designed for handling data storage on paper tape. In those days, floppy disk storage was expensive. The most widely used method of data storage for the microcomputer was paper tape. CP/M was later converted to handle floppy disks. A text editor, assembler, and debugger were also added to allow for the development of machine language programs.

One of the biggest appeals of CP/M is the wide availability of applications software written to run under that operating system. Since conversion of applications software from CP/M-80 to CP/M-86 is relatively simple, it is anticipated that a large volume of software will be available for 16-bit microprocessors running CP/M.

CP/M does present some disadvantages, however. One of these is documentation that many users find difficult to understand. Another disadvantage is that CP/M generally is not as easily mastered by first time computer users as are other operating systems. Finally, CP/M presents certain limitations when working with large capacity hard disk systems.

Digital Research is currently working to overcome these limitations, and expects to announce new versions of CP/M-80 and CP/M-86 sometime in 1982.

UCSD p-System

The UCSD p-System is the third operating system currently available for the IBM PC. The p-System was developed at the Institute for Information Science at the University of California in San Diego in the mid 1970's.

The p-System was first licensed and distributed through the office of the regents of the University of California in the late 1970's. Sole distribution rights were subsequently granted by the office of the regents to SofTech Microsystems, a subsidiary of SofTech Inc.

The p-System is quite different from PC DOS and CP/M-86. While CP/M operates on five different microprocessors (8080, 8085, 8086, 8088, and Z80), and PC DOS operates on five others (Z8000, 68000, 8080, 8086, and 8088), the p-System will operate on over 15 different mini and microcomputer microprocessors.

These include the following:

> Intel 8080, 8085, 8086, 8088
> Digital Equipment LSI-11, PDP-11
> Mos Technology 6502
> Motorola 6800, 6809, 68000
> Texas Instruments 9900
> Zilog Z80, Z8000
> Western Digital Microprocessors

Obviously, the main advantage to the p-System is that programs written under this system will run on a much larger variety of computers than programs written under CP/M-86 or PC DOS.

The "p" in p-System is an abbreviation for **pseudocode.** The pseudocode or **p-code** is the code produced when the programs written in the languages supported by USCD p-System are **compiled.** The three primary languages currently supported under the USCD p-System are PASCAL, FORTRAN, and BASIC.

When a program is written in a version of PASCAL, BASIC, or FORTRAN which is supported under the USCD p-System, that program (whichever the language) is compiled or translated into universal p-code instructions instead of into machine language. The p-code is then translated into machine language by a **P-machine emulator,** which is a program that translates p-code into instructions that can be directly executed by the microprocessor.

Each microprocessor that is supported under the UCSD p-System requires a different P-machine emulator. UCSD p-code uses the same instruction set as is used with Western Digital's microprocessor chips. Therefore, p-code will execute directly with Western Digital microprocessor chips, and no P-machine emulator is required.

The UCSD p-System is then basically unchanged among the different microprocessors supported under the system. The differences lie in the fact that the P-machine emulators are customized for each separate microprocessor.

The obvious advantage to the p-System is the compatibility of programs written under this system. A compiled program written under the p-System for the Apple will run under a PDP-11, Tandy, IBM PC, or any other computer that has a P-machine emulator.

Compiled vs. Interpreted Language

Computer languages are often distinguished as being either **compiled** or **interpreted** languages.

A compiled language program consists of the **source code** and the **compiled code.** The source code consists of the program statements in their original form. For example, the following is a line of source code from a program written in the C-BASIC compiled language:

100 INPUT "ENTER TODAY'S DATE:";DATE.1

The source code is processed by a program known as a **compiler** into the compiled code. The compiled code is very similar to the machine language used by the microprocessor. The compiled code is the code actually used when a compiled program is run. A program known as a **run-time monitor** is used to run the compiled program.

An interpreted language consists of only the source code. The source code is translated line-by-line directly into machine language instructions. The Microsoft BASIC language that is standard on the IBM PC is an interpreted language.

One advantage of interpreted languages over compiled language is that interpreted language programs are more easily developed. When working with interpreted languages, a programmer need only write a program, enter it, run it, and alter it at his own leisure. When working with a compiled language, the source code must be recompiled every time it is edited. This can be frustrating during the program debugging process.

One advantage of compiled languages over interpreted

languages is that the execution time is much faster. The compiled code is much closer to the machine language than the source code. Since interpretation is not necessary, execution of compiled code is much faster.

Monochrome Display

The video display or CRT allows communication between the operator and the computer. The IBM video display, the Monochrome Display, uses a black and white picture tube with a green phosphor to produce a black and green display. A black and green display tends to reduce eye fatigue.

The IBM Monochrome Display is about the same size as a 12 inch black and white television set.

The Monochrome Display gets its power from the System Unit. The AC power cable from the Monochrome Display will connect directly into the power supply outlet located on the rear of the System Unit. This allows the On/Off switch on the System Unit to control the power to both the System Unit and the Monochrome Display.

The Monochrome Display also has a video signal cable which connects into the Monitor/Printer Adapter on the right side of the rear of the System Unit.

The IBM Monochrome Display allows for a display of 25 lines of 80 characters each. The characters output by the IBM Monochrome Display are very sharp and easily read by the operator, thereby preventing eye strain.

The IBM Monochrome Display outputs a character with matrix dimensions of 7 (horizontal) by 9 (vertical) in a 9 by 14 matrix. This additional area allows lower case letters with descenders (such as "y" or "p") to retain their normal appearance.

The characteristics of the IBM Monochrome Display are given in Table 1-9.

Table 1-9. IBM Monochrome Display Features

IBM Monochrome Display	
Size:	Height: 11 inch 280 mm Width: 15 inch 380 mm Depth: 14 inch 350 mm Weight: 17 lbs. 7.9 kg
Video Screen Characteristics:	Diagonal: 11.5 inch 292 mm P-39 Slow Green Phosphor
Cables:	AC Power Cable; Video Cable (with 9 pin D-Connector)
Features:	1. 80 x 25 Display 2. 7 x 9 characters with descenders in a 9 x 14 character box. 3. Direct Drive Video 4. Screen refreshment at 50 Hz; 720 horizontal, 350 vertical resolution.

IBM CPS-80 Printer

The IBM CPS-80 Printer is actually a version of the Epson MX-80 Printer. This printer has an output speed of 80 characters per second in any of several styles of dot matrix print.

The IBM CPS-80 Printer will accept forms with a minimum width of 4 inches and a maximum width of 10 inches. The maximum paper thickness accepted by the IBM printer is 3 plies or .012 inches.

Paper is fed into the IBM printer from the rear of the unit. The unit's ribbon is enclosed in a removable cartridge. Each ribbon has a print capacity of 3 million characters which translates to approximately 10 hours of continuous use.

The IBM printer uses a bidirectional, 9-wire printhead. The printhead has a life expectancy of 30 million impressions. The printhead can easily be replaced by the operator.

A 9 by 9 dot matrix pattern is used to form characters. Character sizes may range from 5 to 16.5 characters per inch (CPI). On an 8 inch line width, these pitch sizes (5, 8.25, 10, and 16.5) will produce a maximum of 40, 66, 80, and 132 characters respectively.

The IBM printer offers three different printing styles; normal, double, and emphasized. Normal printing involves one strike of the print head per character. Double printing involves a double strike of the print head for each character. Emphasized printing involves a single strike for the character after which the paper is stepped up by a fraction of an inch, and a single strike is again made. Emphasized printing gives the appearance of a bold character, which adds to the versatility of the printer.

Printers other than the IBM CPS-80 may be used with the PC. Parallel printers may be connected via either the Monochrome Display/Printer Adapter or the Printer Adapter Cards. Serial printers can be connected via the Asynchronous Communication Adapter.

Table 1-10. IBM CPS-80 Printer Features

IBM CPS-80 Features	
Manufacturers:	Epson America, Inc.
Model No.:	MX-80
Introduction Date:	1979 by Epson
Size:	Height: 4.2 inch 107 mm Width: 14.7 inch 374 mm Depth: 12.0 inch 305 mm Weight: 12 lbs. 5.5 kg
Output Speed:	80 CPS (Characters Per Second)
Interface:	Sprocket feed paper; Minimum width 4 inches 102 mm; Maximum

width 10 inches 254 mm; Maximum thickness 3 ply; .012 inches.

Power: 120 v. AC, 60 Hz - 1 amp maximum

Characteristics:
1. 9-pin dot matrix printhead.
2. Bidirectional printing with logic seeking.
3. 9 x 9 dot characters, 96 ASCII characters, 9 international symbols, 64 graphic characters.
4. Black ribbon cartridge (3 million character life expectancy).
5. Paper-out sensor.
6. Self-Test

Software Controlled Features:
1. Print Sizes:

Name	Pitch	Max char/line
Normal	10	80
Enlarged	5	40
Condensed	16.5	132
Condensed/ Enlarged	8.25	66

2. Print Styles:

Normal: Single strike.

Double: Double strike at same position.

Emphasized: Single strike, stepup paper by 1/216 inches; another strike.

3. Line Spacing: Adjustable to 6, 8, or 10 lines per inch.
4. Horizontal and vertical tabbing.

Serial And Parallel Communications

Data may be sent from the computer to the receiving device (printer or video display) in two different manners; serial and parallel. In parallel communications, the 8 bits representing a character are all sent at one time to the receiving device. In serial communications, each of the 8 bits are sent one at a time to the receiving device.

Monochrome Display/Printer Adapter Card

The Monochrome Display/Printer Adapter Card is used to link the PC to both the Monochrome Display and a parallel printer.

A separate Printer Adapter Card is also available which performs only the parallel printer interface functions of the Monochrome Display/Printer Adapter Card.

The only difference between the combined Display/Printer Adapter and the Printer Adapter Card is the memory location. The starting address for the Display/Printer Adapter and Printer Adapter Cards are separated by 68 locations. Other than different starting memory addresses, the cards operate identically.

The Monochrome Display portion of the combined Display/Printer Adapter Card controls communications between the PC and the video display.

Although the interface to the IBM printer conforms to Centronics electrical standards, the physical connection from the printer to the interface card is made via a DB-25 connector. Centronics, one of the largest printer manufacturers, has established a method of connecting printers to which most manufacturers conform.

To connect a parallel printer to the IBM PC, an IBM Printer Cable must be used. The IBM Printer Cable has a DB-25 connector on one end and a Centronics style connector on the other end. The DB-25 connector is for the System Unit, while the Centronics type connector is for the printer. By using the IBM Printer Cable, the IBM PC can be connected to any parallel printer with a Centronics-style connector.

The reason why the DB-25 connector is used on the PC is to prevent a problem known as **cross-talk.** Cross-talk is a fairly common problem when long cables are used for parallel communication. Cross-talk occurs when the electrical signals from the cable's parallel wires interfere with each other. To eliminate cross-talk, additional wires are placed in the cable that absorb (ground) this troublesome interference.

The Display/Printer Adapter card contains 8K of ROM (which is used to hold the codes for 256 different characters) and 4K of RAM (which holds one full screen of data--80 characters by 25 rows). The display RAM is refreshed 50 times per second.

Two bytes of memory are used for every character displayed in the Display/Printer Adapter (as well as the Color/Graphics Monitor Adapter). The first byte is used to store the ASCII code for the character.

The second byte is known as the **attribute code.** In the Monochrome display, the attribute code controls the following four video features:

1. Darkness of the background
2. Darkness of the foreground
3. Intensity or brightness of the character
4. Blinking or non-blinking character

The attribute byte allows the following six combinations on the Monochrome Display.

1. White character on a dark background (video mode).
2. Dark character on a white background (reverse video).
3. Flashing bright character on a dark foreground.
4. White character on a white background (invisible character).
5. Dark character on a dark background (invisible character).
6. Flashing dark character on a white background.

As mentioned previously, both the Monochrome and Color Adapter allow for 25 lines on the display. Generally, programs are written to use at most 24 lines of the display. The 25th line is known as the **status line.**

The status line generally is used to communicate messages or prompts to the operator. Since programs generally do not use the status line of the display, this line offers an excellent area in which to place prompts and other information directed to the operator.

Table 1-11. IBM Monochrome Display/Printer Adapter Features

IBM Monochrome Display/Printer Adapter
Size: Height: 4 inch 102 mm Width: 14 inch 357 mm Depth: .25 inch 6.3 mm
Location: System Unit Expansion Slot (generally slot 2)

Characteristics: 1. Display
    a. 80 x 25 or 40 x 25 text modes
    b. Normal, reverse, flashing, high-intensity modes
    c. Motorola 6845 CRT controller
    d. 4K RAM (static) display buffer
    e. 8K ROM for 256 character codes
 	
2. Printer
    a. 8-bit parallel port (centronics compatible)
    b. Acknowledge, Busy, Paper Out, and Select signals
    c. Allows use of any Centronics compatible printer device
    d. 12 TTL buffered output points
    e. 5 input ports readable under program control
    f. 25 pin D-connector (female) used

The Monochrome Display/Printer Adapter uses the Motorola 6845 CRT Controller to interface to the video display (as does the Color/Graphics Monitor Adapter). The 6845 is software controlled. This means that a program can directly control the output to the screen. For example, a program could be implemented to restrict the screen area to a size smaller than 25 x 80.

Color Graphics Monitor Adapter

The main difference between the Color/Graphics Monitor Adapter and the Display/Printer Adapter is that the Color/Graphics board can provide for color, while the Display/Printer board cannot.

The Color/Graphics Monitor Adapter can be used with a color monitor or a color television set when an RF modulator is supplied.

The Color/Graphics Adapter operates under two principal methods of operation; the **alphanumeric (A/N)** or text mode and the **all points addressable (APA)** graphics mode. Each of these two primary modes includes several secondary operating modes.

A/N Mode

The A/N mode operates with a video output of 25 lines of 40 characters each when used with a television set, low-resolution monitor, or high resolution monitor. A video output of 25 lines of 80 characters each is available with high resolution monitors.

In the monochrome mode of the A/N mode, characters can be displayed in reverse, high intensity, and blinking formats. In the color mode, up to 16 foreground (or character colors) can be supported on any one of eight background colors. The color mode also supports blinking characters.

The colors that may be attained through the use of the Color/Graphics Adapter are listed in Table 1-12. The numbers used in BASIC to attain the color are given in column 1. The primary colors which make up the color are given in the last four columns of Table 1-12.

The sixteen colors that can be obtained are all combinations of the three primary colors (red, green, and blue), and the intensity signal. Electronic color mixing is somewhat different from photographic color mixing, in that green, not yellow, is the third primary color.

The three primary colors produce eight different colors (0 to 7 in Table 1-12.). The intensity signal results in a difficult tint for each of these eight colors (8 to 15 in Table 1-12.).

Colors 8 through 15 in Table 1-12 may not be available with certain monitors or televisions that cannot detect the intensity control.

Table 1-12. Color/Graphics Adapter Available Colors

Color No.	Color Name	Red	Green	Blue	Intensity Signal
0	Black	N	N	N	N
1	Blue	N	N	Y	N
2	Green	N	Y	N	N
3	Cyan	N	Y	Y	N
4	Red	Y	N	N	N
5	Magenta	Y	N	Y	N
6	Brown	Y	Y	N	N
7	Light Grey	Y	Y	Y	N
8	Dark Grey	N	N	N	Y
9	Light Blue	N	Y	N	Y
10	Light Green	N	Y	N	Y
11	Light Cyan	N	Y	Y	Y
12	Light Red	Y	N	N	Y
13	Light Magenta	Y	N	Y	Y
14	Yellow	Y	Y	Y	Y
15	White	Y	Y	Y	Y

Y = Yes   N = No
Colors 8 through 15 may not be available on some monitors and televisions.

APA Mode

The APA (all points addressable) mode allows a program to control each dot on the video display. The APA primary mode supports three secondary modes; the **high resolution, medium resolution,** and **low resolution** modes.

In the high resolution mode, the screen is divided into 640 dots horizontally by 200 dots vertically. Medium resolution consists of 320 dots horizontally by 200 dots vertically. Low resolution consists of 160 dots horizontally by 200 dots vertically.

Video Devices For The Color/Graphics Monitor Adapter

Four types of video devices can be used with the Color/Graphics Monitor Adapter; a television set, a B&W monitor, a color monitor, or an RGB color monitor.

An **RF modulator** must be used to connect a television set to the Color/Graphics Monitor Adapter. The RF modulator is a device which converts video signals into TV channels.

When using a television set for video output, only the 40 by 25 mode can be used. The 80 x 25 screen format is not available.

Asynchronous Communications Adapter

The asynchronous communications adapter allows the IBM PC to communicate with other devices, such as other computers, printers, and modems.

Asynchronous communication refers to a method of data transmission, whereby information is sent to the receiving device one bit at a time with additional information included which gives the starting and stopping points of each character. In other words, asynchronous communication consists of sending data in serial form from sending device to receiving device at non-standard timing intervals.

The asynchronous communications adapter can be placed in any one of the five expansion slots. The adapter includes a DB-25 (25 pin) connector that extends from the rear of the System Unit.

The features of the Asynchronous Communications Adapter are listed in Table 1-13.

Table 1-13. Asynchronous Communications Adapter

IBM Asynchronous Communications Adapter	
Size:	Height: 4 inch 102 mm Width: 5 inch 127 mm Depth: .25 inch
Components:	1. INS 8250 Asynchronous Communications Element (ACE) 2. ACE Support Circuiting 3. DB-25 connector on card extending from rear of system unit 4. Jumper block for RS-232C or 25 ma. current loop (TTY compatible)
Characteristics:	1. Fully software controllable 2. 50-9600 baud

Keyboard Usage

The IBM keyboard layout is depicted in Illustration 1-10. Note that the keys outlined in grey are the same as those used on a typewriter.

In Illustration 1-11, the keys outlined in grey are keys used in writing or running programs. These are explained in Table 1-14.

In Illustration 1-12, the program function keys are outlined in grey. These are used to instruct your PC to perform certain commands. These are listed in Table 1-15.

In Illustration 1-13, the numeric keypad keys are outlined in grey. The NUMLOCK key means number lock. When this key is depressed, the numeric keypad is activated. The various numeric keypad keys are discussed in Table 1-16.

Illustration 1-10. IBM Keyboard (Typewriter Keys)

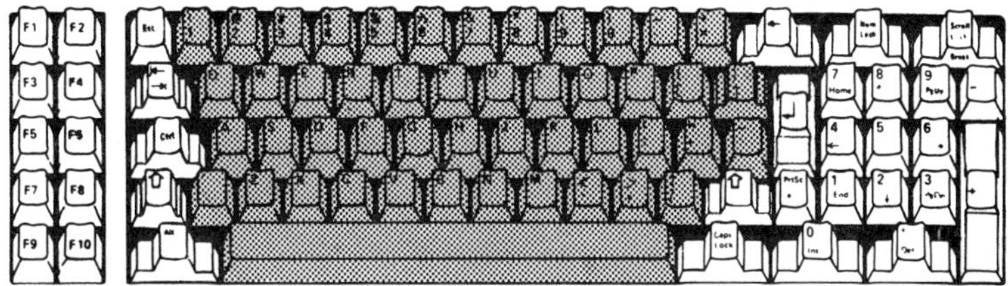

Illustration 1-11. IBM Keyboard (Program Control Keys)

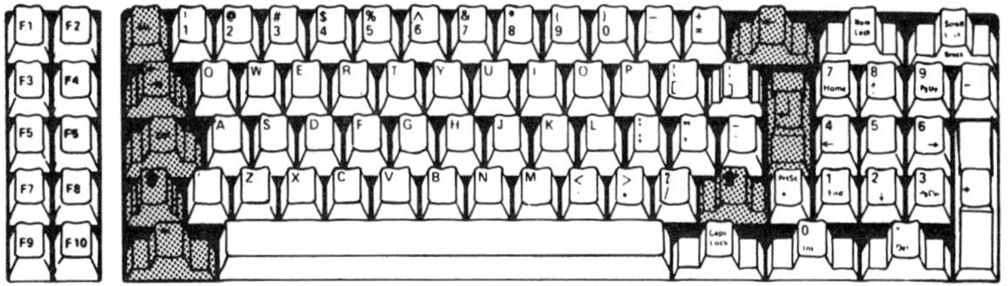

Table 1-14. Program Control Keys

Key	Explanation
ESC	**Escape Key**--removes the last line that the cursor is in. However, the line is not deleted from memory.
⊢← →⊣	**Tab Key**--performs a tab function much as on a typewriter. Tabs are set after every 8th character.
CTRL	**Control Key**--used in conjunction with another to perform a command or a function.
⇧	**Shift Key**--used to change lower case letters to capitals.
ALT	**Alternate Key**--used with alpha typing keys to enter BASIC keywords.
←	**Backspace Key**--used to move the cursor one charcter to the left whenever the key is pressed.
↵	**Enter Key**--used to move cursor from final character position on a line to the first position on the next line.

Illustration 1-12. IBM Keyboard (Program Function Keys)

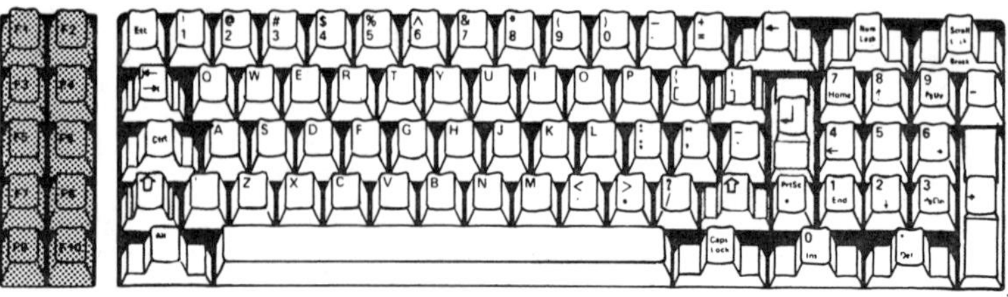

Table 1-15. Program Function Keys

Key	Explanation
F1	**LIST Function**--is used to display the lines of your program on the screen.
F2	**RUN Function**--is used to execute a program from its beginning.
F3	**LOAD Function**--is used to read a program from a storage device (ex. cassette tape) and store it in main memory.
F4	**SAVE Function**--is used to store a program on a storage device from memory.
F5	**CONT Function**--is used to restart a program after it has been temporarily interrupted by a STOP or CTRL BREAK.
F6	**LPT1: Function**--is used to transfer data from the video screen to the line printer.
F7	**TRON Function**--refers to trace on. This function causes the line numbers of program lines to be displayed as these lines are executed.
F8	**TROFF Function**--refers to trace off. This function cancels function F7.
F9	**KEY Function**--is used to change the function of the other 9 function keys.
F10	**SCREEN Function**--is used to return a program to the character mode from the graphics mode and also turn off the color.

Illustration 1-13. IBM Keyboard (Numeric Keyboard Keys)

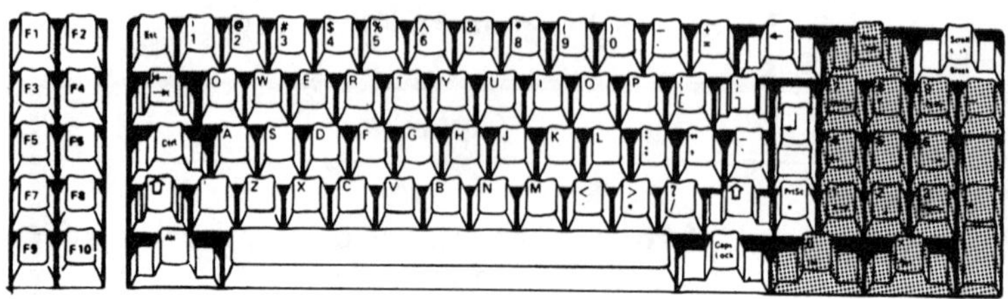

Table 1-16. Numeric Keypad Keys (NUMLOCK Key Depressed)

Key	Explanation
1-9	When the NUMLOCK key is depressed, keys 1 through 9 will be functioning.
. DEL	When the NUMLOCK key is depressed the decimal point will be used.
0 INS	When the NUMLOCK key is depressed, the zero will be used.
−	The Minus key is used with the numeric keypad.
+	The Plus key is used with the numeric keypad.

When the NUMLOCK key is released, the numeric keypad will be cancelled. The same keys outlined in Illustration 1-13 will retain different meanings which will be discussed in Table 1-17.

**Table 1-17. Non-Numeric Keypad Keys
(NUMLOCK Key Released)**

Key	Explanation
7 HOME	The Home key moves the cursor to the first character position in the top line on the screen.
8 ↑	The Up Arrow key moves the cursor up one line every time it is pressed.
4 ←	The Left Arrow key moves the cursor to the left by one position every time it is pressed.
6 →	The Right Arrow key moves the cursor to the right by one position every time it is pressed.
2 ↓	The Down Arrow key moves the cursor down by one line every time it is pressed.
1 END	The End key moves the cursor to the final character on the line.
● DEL	The DEL key deletes the character where the cursor is presently positioned.
0 INS	The Insert key is used to set the keyboard into the insert mode. In the insert mode, any data entries will be made at the current cursor position and all data to the right of the cursor position will move to the right. The insert mode is exited by pressing the Insert key a second time.

The miscellaneous keys are outlined in grey in Illustration 1-14. These are described in Table 1-18.

Illustration 1-14. IBM Keyboard (Miscellaneous Keys)

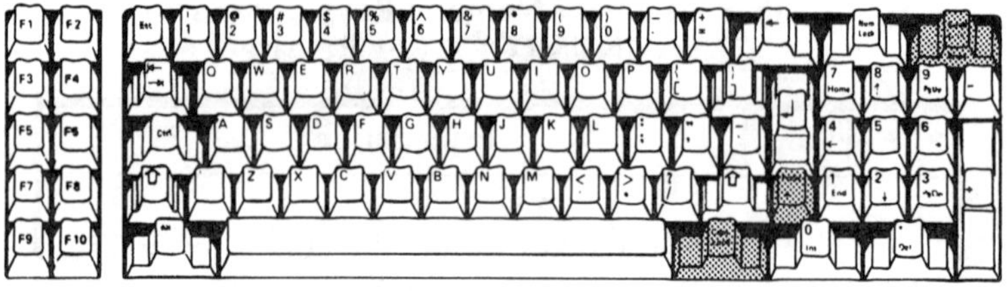

Table 1-18. Miscellaneous Keys

Key	Explanation
CAPS LOCK	Like the NUMLOCK key, the CAPS LOCK key is a toggle key. When it is depressed, the letters will be typed in capitals (upper case). When it is released, the letters will be typed in lower case.
PRT SC *	The PRT SC (or Print Screen) key prints an * with the SHIFT key released. When SHIFT is depressed, the PRT SC key will cause all data to be printed to the screen.
SCR LOCK BREAK	The SCR LOCK (Scroll Lock/Break) key is used in the unshift mode with the Control key to stop a program from running.

The Control key can be used in conjunction with other keys to create certain functions. These are listed in Table 1-19. Note that the Control key must be pressed simultaneously with the other key(s).

Table 1-19. Control Key Combinations

Control Key Combination	Explanation
CTRL + SCROLL LOCK/BREAK = BREAK	This combination can be used to stop a program while it is running, and to identify the line number where it stops.
CTRL + NUMLOCK = PAUSE	This combination is used to stop your program from running. The program will continue when any key is pressed.
CTRL + → = TAB	This combination moves the cursor to the next word on the current line.
CTRL + ← = REVERSE TAB	This combination moves the cursor to the preceding word on the current line.
CTRL + HOME = CLEAR SCREEN	This combination erases all data from the screen and then moves the cursor to the upper left hand corner.
CTRL + ALT + DEL = SYSTEM RESET	If the Control and ALT keys are simultaneously pressed while the Delete key is pressed, the PC's operating system will be reloaded.

Keyboard Usage Under DOS

Some of the keys and Control key combinations have meanings specific to the IBM DOS operating system. These are listed in Table 1-20.

Table 1-20. DOS Key Usage

Key	Explanation
F1	This function key can be used under DOS to redisplay a line that was previously entered, one character at a time.
F2 + Character	When F2 is entered followed by a character, all of the previously entered lines will be displayed up to the first occurrence of the character following F2.
F3	This function key is used to redisplay the line previously entered.
F4 + Character	When F4 is entered followed by a character, the screen will skip all of the characters in the line previously entered up to the character entered after F4.
F5	This function key is used to save the line currently being displayed for further editing.
CTRL + NUMLOCK = SUSPEND	This combination suspends system operation so that the user can read the display. Press any key to continue operation.
CTRL + PRT SC = ECHO	This combination echoes and prints whatever the user types and whatever is displayed by the system. To shut off this procedure, press CTRL + PRT SC again.
CTRL + SCR LOCK/BREAK = BREAK	This combination is used to stop your command program while it is running.

IBM Printer Operation

The IBM 80 CPS Matrix Printer will work with nearly every computer that uses a parallel interface. The IBM Printer will accept the 96 ASCII characters and symbols as well as the 64 graphic code characters. These characters can be printed in any size desired; condensed, enlarged, emphasized, and normal.

Control Switches And Lights

The various control switches and lights for the IBM Printer are shown in Illustration 1-15, and are discussed below.

Power Switch--This switch controls the power to the printer. When it is on, the printer will be on and the power light on the control panel will be on.

Ready Light--This light will be on when the printer is ready to receive data.

Paper Out Light--This light will be on when the paper supply is near its end. The printer will also enact a beep as a warning.

On Line Light--This light will be on when the power switch is first turned on.

On Line Switch--This switch controls the on line mode. If this switch is pressed once, the printer will go to off line status, and will not be able to receive data from the computer. If the on line switch is pressed a second time, the printer will return to the on line mode.

Form Feed--This switch can only be used when the printer is off line. When this switch is pressed, the paper will be fed to the next top-of-form position.

Top-of-form can be set by adjusting the form to the first print line before the printer is powered on. Once the printer has been turned on, the printer will automatically feed to the current print position whenever the form feed switch is pressed.

Line Feed--This switch is only active when the printer is off line. When this switch is pressed, the printer will advance the form by one line. If this switch is pressed and then held, the form will continue to advance until the switch has been released.

Illustration 1-15. IBM Printer Control Switches And Lights

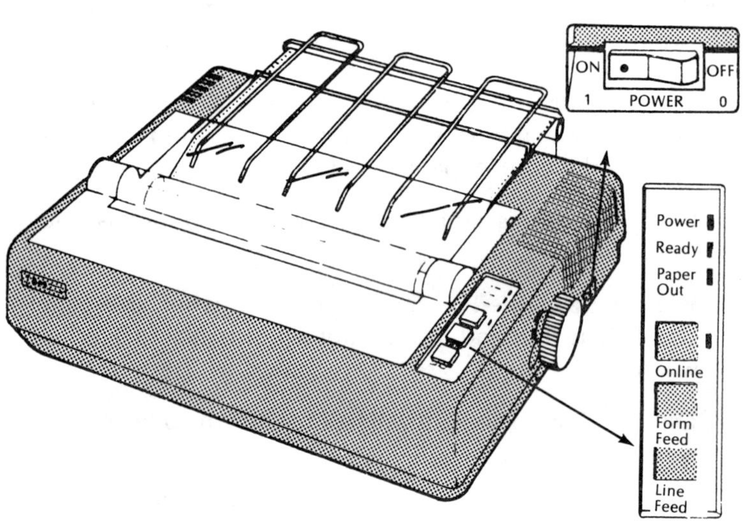

PC Start-Up Procedure — Diskette System

If you purchased your IBM Personal Computer with one or more optional disk drives, you should have received a copy of DOS-- IBM's disk operating system. Do not use your master copy of DOS for everyday use. Make copies of the master, and use these copies for everyday use.

To start-up DOS, first insert a copy of the DOS diskette in the diskette drive on the left side of the PC. During insertion, the label side of the diskette should be facing up. Keep inserting the diskette until you hear a click. Then, close the lever over the diskette drive.

Next, turn on the power to the monitor and printer (if connected), and finally turn on the power to the System Unit. The following message will be displayed:

Enter today's date (m-d-y):

Once the date has been entered, the display will resemble that shown in Illustration 1-16.

The prompt (A>) indicates which is your current drive (in this case--drive A).

Next, type in the following:

A> <u>BASIC</u> 

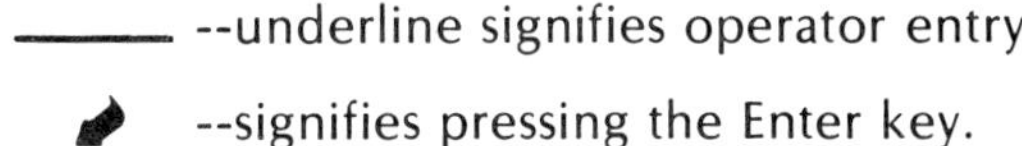

      --underline signifies operator entry

      --signifies pressing the Enter key.

Illustration 1-16. DOS Start-Up Display

```
Enter today's date (m-d-y): 6/24/82
The IBM Personal Computer DOS
Version 1.00   Copyright IBM Corp. 1981

A> ___
```

The display will then resemble that shown in Illustration 1-17.

Illustration 1-17. BASIC Start-Up Display

```
The IBM Personal Computer BASIC
Version D 1.00 Copyright IBM Corp. 1981
xxxxx Bytes Free
Ok
___
```

If the user wishes to start Advanced BASIC rather than Diskette BASIC, he can do so by entering BASICA rather than BASIC. All other procedures are the same.

The Ok is known as the IBM BASIC prompt. The prompt indicates that BASIC commands or programs can be entered. The cursor appears beneath the BASIC prompt.

PC Start-Up Procedure--Non-Diskette System

If your IBM Personal Computer does not have any optional disk drives, all that is needed for start-up is to turn on the power switch. The video display will resemble that shown in Illustration 1-17. Once the BASIC prompt (Ok) appears, the user can begin entering BASIC commands or programs.

BASIC Command Entry — DOS

If you are a beginning programmer, this section may seem a bit confusing. If so, skip this section and continue with Chapter 2.

When you are loading Disk or Advanced BASIC, additional parameters can be included with the BASIC or BASICA entry. These parameters can be used for the following purposes:

Set aside storage areas for programs and data.

Set aside storage area for buffers.

Instruct BASIC to load and run a program.

The configuration for the BASIC command with all of its optional parameters is as follows.

    BASIC [A] [*filespec*] [/F:*files*] [/S:*bufsize*] [/C:*bufcom*]
        [/M:*work area*]

The optional parameter **filespec** indicates the file specification of a program that is to be automatically loaded and executed by BASIC. If no filename extension is specified, the extension .BAS will be supplied.

The optional parameter /F:*files* indicates the maximum number of files that are allowed to be open at one time while a BASIC program is being executed. The maximum number allowed is 15. If this parameter is omitted, the number of files open will default to 3.

The optional parameter /S:*bufsize* assigns the buffer size to be used with random files. The default value for the buffer size is 128. The maximum size that may be used is 32767. For maximum performance, IBM recommends that you use a buffer size of 512 bytes for random file buffer size. Note that the record length parameter used with the OPEN statement may not be greater than the number of bytes specified in /S:*bufsize*.

The optional parameter /C:*bufcom* is used to initialize the area to be reserved for the communications receive buffer. This parameter is not used unless the Asychronous Communications Adapter is installed on your system. The default value for this parameter is 256 bytes for the receive buffer and 128 bytes for the transmit buffer. IBM recommends that the value /C:1024 be used for high speed lines. If a value of /C:0 is specified, no buffer space will be reserved for communications. In this case, communications support will be disabled when BASIC is loaded.

The optional parameter/M:*work area* can be used to initialize the maximum amount of memory in bytes that can be used as a workarea under BASIC. The maximum value that can be used is 64K. The default value is 64K. This parameter is often used to reserve work areas for machine language subroutines.

When specifying these optional parameters (*files, bufsize, bufcom,* and *work area*), a decimal, octal, or hexadecimal number must be used. Octal number entries must be preceded by &O and hexadecimal number entries must be preceded by &H.

CHAPTER 2.
INTRODUCTION TO BASIC

Communication between humans and computers is accomplished in the same manner in which communication is accomplished between humans--with the use of languages. Hundreds of languages have been developed for use with computers. BASIC, which is an abbreviation for Beginner's All-Purpose Symbolic Language, is the most widely used language for microcomputers.

Many first-time computer users have the mistaken idea that their computer has the ability to think. This is, of course, untrue. A computer can only do what it is instructed. It can do nothing on its own. The user must inform the computer exactly what it is to do with a set of instructions. These instructions are known as a **program.**

In this chapter, as well as the following chapters, we will concentrate on learning to write programs for the IBM Personal Computer in the BASIC language.

Versions of IBM BASIC

The IBM PC uses a version of BASIC known as Microsoft BASIC. As mentioned in Chapter 1, three separate variations of Microsoft BASIC are available, depending upon your system configuration. These are Cassette BASIC, Diskette BASIC, and Advanced BASIC.

Cassette BASIC is the most elementary form of Microsoft BASIC used on the PC. Cassette BASIC is furnished with all IBM PC's on ROM.

Diskette BASIC is furnished on diskette for PC's with a diskette drive. Diskette BASIC includes all of the commands in Cassette BASIC as well as additional commands that allow the usage of disk drives. These commands will be covered in more detail in Chapter 5.

Advanced BASIC is the most advanced form of BASIC used with the PC. Advanced BASIC includes all of the commands of Diskette BASIC as well as additional commands that allow the operator to use advanced graphics functions, play music, and control options such as a light pen and game paddles. Advanced BASIC is only available with computers that contain the color/graphics interface.

In this book, we will distinguish between those commands which are exclusive to Diskette BASIC and Advanced BASIC. Remember, all Cassette BASIC commands are included in both Diskette and Advanced BASIC, and all Diskette commands are included in Advanced BASIC.

Command & Execute Mode

Programming can be accomplished in either of two modes with the IBM Personal Computer, command or execute. The **command** mode is active when the prompt, Ok, is displayed on the screen. In the command mode, program lines entered by the user are not immediately executed. These are stored in RAM until the user specifies what the final disposition of the program is to be.

Program statements entered in the command mode must be assigned unique **line numbers.** These line numbers are used by the program to identify the program statements.

The **execute** mode is active when the RUN command is executed. The execute mode can be used to run programs entered under the command mode. Once the program has been run, the computer reverts to the command mode, and the Ok prompt is displayed. This is shown in Illustration 2-1.

Illustration 2-1. Command & Execute Modes

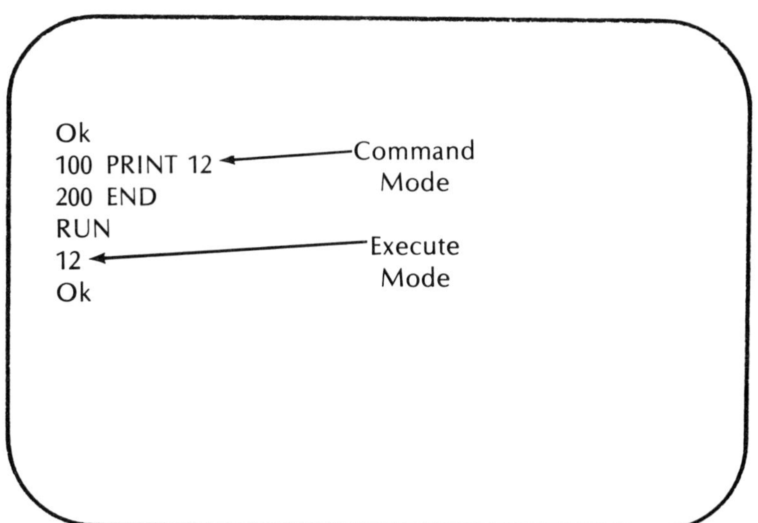

Entering A Program

In the preceding section, we touched upon the fundamentals of entering and running a BASIC program on the IBM PC. In this section, we will expand upon that discussion using the example in Illustration 2-2.

Note that in the first 5 lines of Illustration 2-2, a program was entered in the command mode and run in the execute mode. After the answer, 5.0, has been displayed, the Ok prompt appears.

At this point the original program is stored in RAM, and can be run again if desired. Also, the program being held in RAM can be added to or changed. That is what was done in line number 150 of Illustration 2-2. An additional statement was inserted between statements 100 and 200 in the program being stored in RAM. This revised program can be executed by again entering RUN.

Illustration 2-2. Entering And Running A Program

```
Ok
100  PRINT 5
200  END
RUN
 5
Ok
150  PRINT -5
RUN
 5
-5
Ok
NEW
Ok
100  PRINT 50
200  END
RUN
 50
Ok
```

RAM can only hold one program at a time. The NEW command is used to erase the program in memory so as to allow a new program to be entered. Note the use of NEW in Illustration 2-2.

Note in our examples the following features common to the BASIC programs:

1) Each program line must begin with a line number. The computer executes program lines in order from lowest line number to highest line number.

2) The END statement signals the end of a program. When END is executed, the program run will stop and the Ok prompt will be displayed.

It is recommended that consecutive line numbers (i.e. 1, 2, 3, 4, 5, etc.) not be used in a program. By using line numbers which are a fixed multiple (i.e. 100, 200, 300, 400, etc.), additional line numbers can be inserted between existing lines without renumbering the line numbers.

Line numbers need not be entered in any particular order. For example, the user could enter lines 100 and 200 and then enter line 150. The computer will automatically rearrange the lines according to their line numbers.

Finally, if the user enters two lines with the same line number, the computer will erase the first line and replace it with the second. This feature allows the user to replace an entire line by merely entering a new line with the same line number.

BASIC Constants

In BASIC, constants can be defined as data items with fixed values. Constants may either be numeric or string. Numeric constants consist of numbers as shown in the example below:

$$7, -5, 4.99872, 8714321$$

String constants consist of a group of keyboard characters. These may be letters, numbers, or any other keyboard symbol. String constants are surrounded by a pair of quotation marks as shown in the example below:

"John Doe", "Total is $29.95", "Chicago, IL 60636"

Even though numbers may appear within a string constant, these numbers cannot be used for calculations.

BASIC Variables

A variable can be defined as a quantity that can assume any one of a group of values. Variables are represented by variable names. These consist of a letter followed optionally by additional letters and/or numbers. The value assumed by a variable is subject to change depending upon the program statement being executed. For example, in the following,

```
100  LET A = 5.0
200  LET B = 7.0
300  LET A = A+B
```

the variable A is initially assigned a value of 5.0 and B is assigned a value of 7.0. In line 300, the variable A is assigned a new value equal to the sum of variable A and B, which is 12.0. The previous value of A is erased.

Note the use of the LET statement in the preceding example. The LET statement is used to assign a value to a variable. Whenever a LET statement is used in a program, the value of the variable on the left side of the equation is to be replaced with the value appearing on the right.

The reserved word, LET, need not actually be included in a LET statement. Both of the following statements have the same meaning:

```
100  LET A = 5
200  A = 5
```

BASIC Variable Names

IBM BASIC allows any group of up to 40 characters to be used as a variable name--as long as the first character of the group is a letter of the alphabet and as long as the variable name does not duplicate a reserved word (see Appendix A). Examples of reserved words are:

LET, GOTO, IF, READ, DATA

The following are examples of valid BASIC variable names:

```
A                JOHN
B23456           N4N
TOTAL.DATA       B%
A2               N
```

while the following are invalid variable names:

2BB7	END
1A	FOR
PRINT	CLS

All of the preceding examples of valid variable names should be used to represent numeric data. Variable names can also be used to represent string data. These are known as string variables. String variable names consist of a valid variable name followed by the dollar sign ($). The following are examples of valid string variable names:

A$	NEW.DATE$
ZIP$	MONTH7$
A7$	N222$

Integer, Single-Precision, and Double-Precision Data

Numeric data can be classified in IBM BASIC as **integer, single-precision,** and **double-precision.** An integer is a counting or whole number as shown in the following examples:

$$7, 8, 1, -1, 14, 17, 32, 978, -111$$

An integer type variable can be used to represent integer constants. (Integer constants can also be represented with numeric variables.) An integer variable name consists of a valid variable name followed by the percent symbol (%). The following are examples of valid integer variable names.

$$Z1\%, TOTAL\%, A\%, N1234\%$$

When a value is set for an integer variable, any fractional portion of that value will be **truncated** (dropped). For example, in the following example, A% will be set at 7.

$$100 \ \ LET \ A\% = 7.89$$

A **single-precision** value consists of a numeric value with a maximum of seven digits. Any additional digits are truncated beginning with the least significant digits. A single-precision variable name consists of a legal variable name followed by the symbol '!'. Also, any variable name used without a type designation character (ex. A2, B, CCC, D29) is assumed to be a single-precision type variable.

A **double-precision** value consists of a numeric value with a maximum of seventeen digits. Any additional digits are truncated beginning with the least significant digits. A double-precision variable name consists of a legal variable name followed by the symbol '#'.

Finally, remember that variable names with different type identifiers are regarded by BASIC as completely unique variables. In other words, all of the following variable names:

A$, A#, A, A%

identify separate, unique variables.

CHAPTER 3.
BEGINNING IBM BASIC

Introduction

In this chapter, we will expand on the concepts used in BASIC and the fundamentals of BASIC programming. We will discuss the structure of a BASIC statement, arithmetic and logical operations, the use of the Remark statement, elementary input and output programming, branching statement, index variables, and loops.

BASIC Statement Structure

Every statement in IBM BASIC must contain at least one **key** or **reserved** word. A key word identifies the calculation, decision, input, or output function to be performed. The key words are described individually in Chapter 7 and are listed in alphabetical order in Appendix A.

In addition to key words, numeric constants, string constants, variables, and special symbols may appear in a BASIC statement. These are known as the statement **parameters.**

BASIC commands may be entered in upper case, lower case, or a mixture of both. Wherever the user is allowed to insert a blank space in a statement, he may insert as many additional blank spaces as desired. The extra spaces will be ignored.

Be certain that blank spaces are included where required. For example, the following,

```
PRINT "JOHN"
PRINT"JOHN"
```

have completely different meanings.

In BASIC, key words, punctuation marks, line numbers, and blank spaces must be placed in their proper order. When these are out of order, a syntax error will occur. These will be discussed in Chapter 6.

The user can elect to place several BASIC statements on a single line. This is accomplished by separating the statements appearing on the same line with a colon (:). For example, the following statements,

```
100  LET  A% = 10
200  LET  B% = 20
300  LET  C% = 30
```

could be combined into a single statement as shown below:

```
100  LET  A% = 10: B% = 20: C% = 30
```

Arithmetic Operations

The symbols used for addition, subtraction, multiplication, division, and exponentiation are known as **arithmetic operators** in BASIC. The symbols + and – are used for addition and subtraction respectively. The asterisk (*) is used to indicate multiplication, while the slash (/) is used to indicate division.

When a + or – sign precedes a number, the symbol is used to specify that number's sign. When + or – is used to change a number's sign, that usage is known as a unary operation. Unary operators can be used to change the sign of a numeric constant or variable as shown below:

```
100  LET  A = -A
```

When unary operators are used in the manner shown above, the unary operation is regarded as an arithmetic operation.

The term **arithmetic expression** is used to describe the use of an arithmetic operator with numeric constants and/or variables. The following are examples of arithmetic expressions.

$$X + Y + 7.0$$
$$100/A + B$$
$$3000 * 10 + 1$$

Exponentiation

Exponentiation is the process of raising a number to a specified power. For example, in the following,

$$A^5$$

the numeric variable A would be evaluated as:

$$A * A * A * A * A$$

In IBM BASIC, exponentiation is indicated with the caret symbol, ^. This symbol is produced by the 6 key with the keyboard in the shift position.

Exponentiation can be used in an arithmetic expression as shown below:

$$8 * 3 + 7^2$$

The preceding expression would evaluate to 73.

Mixing Variable Types In Arithmetic Expressions

Although certain variable types may be mixed in an IBM expression, it is preferable to use a single variable type throughout each expression. By doing so, execution time will be decreased, memory requirements will be reduced, and the probability for program errors will also be reduced.

An example of mixing different numeric types in the same expression is given below:

$$A = B + 1$$

Both A and B are single-precision numeric variables, while 1 is an integer constant. The integer constant must be converted to a real number (as shown below), before the expression can be evaluated.

$$A = B + 1.0$$

When numeric variables are used in expressions, the variable on the left side of the equal sign is assigned the value of the expression on the right side. The value on the right side of the expression will be converted to the value specified by the numeric variable on the left side. For instance, in the following,

$$A\% = 1.03 + 2.07$$

the value on the left side of the expression 3.1 will be converted to the integer 3 so that it agrees with the integer variable A%. If A% were replaced with A, no conversion would have been necessary.

Order Of Evaluation — Arithmetic Operators

When an expression is evaluated in IBM BASIC, certain arithmetic operators have priorities over others.

The arithmetic operators are listed in Table 3-1 in their order of evaluation.

Most of the arithmetic operators will already be familiar to you. However, two of them, integer division and Modulo arithmetic, may not be familiar.

In integer division, the operand is rounded to an integer value before the division is performed. The quotient is also truncated to an integer. For example, in the following expression,

$$A = 37.98 \setminus 7.87$$

A would evaluate to 4.

Table 3-1. Order of Evaluation (Arithmetic Operators)

Symbol	Operation	Example
^	Exponentiation	A ^ B
–	Negation	–A
*	Multiplication	A*B
/	Floating Point Division	A/B
\	Integer Division	A\B
MOD	Modulo Arithmetic	A MOD B
+	Addition	A + B
–	Subtraction	A – B

Modulo arithmetic gives the integer value that is the remainder of an integer division operator. In the following expression,

$$A = 10 \text{ MOD } 3$$

A would evaluate to 1.

In an expression with more than one arithmetic operator, the operators with higher priority are evaluated first followed by those with lower priority. Evaluation is accomplished from left to right in the expression. The following is an example of the evaluation of the arithmetic operators in an expression:

$$A = 37.1 + 12.9 * 2.1 + 7 - 4\,{}^\wedge 2$$
$$= 37.1 + 12.9 * 2.1 + 7 - 16$$
$$= 37.1 + 27.09 + 7 - 16$$
$$= 55.19$$

Parentheses can be used to alter the order of evaluation in arithmetic expressions. Expressions appearing within parentheses have the highest priority in the order of evaluation. For example, the use of parentheses when used with our preceding example could change the value of the expression.

$$A = (37.1 + 12.9) * 2.1 + (7 - 4)\,{}^\wedge 2$$
$$= 50.0 * 2.1 + 3\,{}^\wedge 2$$
$$= 50.0 * 2.1 + 9$$
$$= 105.0 + 9$$
$$= 114.0$$

Relational Operators

The following relational operators are used in IBM BASIC:

```
 <  or LT  ->  less than
<= or LE  ->  less than or equal to
 >  or GT  ->  greater than
>= or GE  ->  greater than or equal to
 =  or EQ  ->  equal to
<> or NE  ->  not equal
```

A relational operation evaluates to either true or false. For example, if the constant 1.0 was compared to the constant 2.0 to see whether they were equal, the expression would evaluate to false. In BASIC, a value of −1 represents a condition of true, while a value of 0 represents false.

The only values returned by a comparison in BASIC are –1 (true) or 0 (false). These values can be used as any other integer would be used. The following results are generated by the following relational expressions:

$$5 \text{ GT } 7 \longrightarrow 0 \text{ (false)}$$
$$5 \text{ GT } 3 \longrightarrow -1 \text{ (true)}$$
$$7 \text{ LE } 7 \longrightarrow -1 \text{ (true)}$$

Relational operations are evaluated after the addition and subtraction arithmetic operations. The order of evaluation of the relational operators is given in Table 3-2.

Although different numeric data types may be compared in a relational expression (ex. integer to single-precision), numeric and string data may not be compared.

Table 3-2. Order Of Evaluation (Relational Operators)

Symbol	Operation	Example
=	Equality	A = B
<>or><	Inequality	A<>B; A><B
<	Less Than	A<B
>	Greater Than	A>B
<= or =<	Less Than or Equal To	A<= B; A =<B
>= or =>	Greater Than or Equal To	A>= B; A => B

Relational operations using numeric operations are fairly straightforward. However, relational operations using string values may prove confusing to the first-time computer user. Strings are compared by taking the ASCII value for each character in the string one at a time and comparing the codes.

If the strings are of the same length, then the string containing the first character with a lower code number is the lesser. If the length of the strings are unequal, then the shorter string is the lesser. Blank spaces are counted and have an ASCII value of 32.

The following comparisons between strings would evaluate as true.

```
"ABC" = "ABC"
"ABC  ">"ABC"
"aAA">"AAA"
"Alfred"<"Zachary"
A$<Z$ where A$ = "Alfred" and Z$ = "Zachary"
```

Note that all string constants must be enclosed in quotation marks when used as constants.

Remark Statements

Remark statements are used in programs to provide an explanation of the program logic. Remark statements may be inserted wherever desired in a BASIC program. A Remark statement can be designated with the keyword REM as shown below:

```
100  REM CALCULATE TOTAL PAY
```

A Remark statement may also be designated with an apostrophe:

```
100 TOTAL = RATE * HOURS ' CALCULATE TOTAL PAY
```

All characters appearing after the apostrophe will be assumed to be part of the Remark statement.

Remark statements are not actually executed. They are inserted merely as an aid in documenting the program.

Outputting Data

In some of our previous examples, we touched upon the use of the PRINT statement to display data. The PRINT statement can be used to display both numeric and string data.

The following program statement,

        100 PRINT "Vendor List"

would display the following on the console:

        Vendor List

Several strings can be displayed on the same line with a single PRINT statement by separating the string constants or variables in the PRINT statement with commas. The following statements,

        100 LET A$ = "JOHN"
        200 PRINT A$, "BILL", "PETER"

would result in the display shown below:

        JOHN   BILL   PETER

IBM BASIC divides the spacing on a line into a series of print zones. Each print zone contains 14 spaces. When a comma appears in a PRINT statement, the computer is instructed to begin printing the next parameter in the PRINT statement at the beginning of the next print zone. In our example above, JOHN would begin in column 1 (print zone 1); BILL in column 15 (print zone 2); and PETER in column 29 (print zone 3).

In this section, we have only discussed sending output to the video display. Output can also be sent to the printer. This is accomplished by using the LPRINT statement in place of PRINT.

If the user wishes to send data to both the screen and printer, it is necessary to use both the PRINT and the LPRINT statements. In the following example,

```
100  A$ = "REPORT TITLE"
200  PRINT A$ : LPRINT A$
```

A$ will be output to both the screen and the printer.

The use of PRINT and LPRINT will be discussed in more detail in Chapter 4.

Inputting Data

Data can be input into the computer while a program is being executed. This is accomplished with the INPUT statement. For example, when the following statement is executed,

```
100  INPUT A
```

the computer will display a question mark and wait for the operator to enter a response. That entry will be assigned to the variable A. The entry must be ended by pressing the Enter key. Program execution will then resume.

The values of several variables can be input with a single INPUT statement. These variables may either be numeric or string as shown in the following example:

```
100  INPUT A$, B$, C
```

When the preceding INPUT statement is executed, the INPUT prompt (?) will be displayed. The operator should then input the data items for variables A$, B$, and C. Each input should be separated by a comma. The Enter key should be pressed after all input entries have been made. An example of a valid entry for the preceding INPUT statement is given below:

```
JOHN, SMITH, 281
```

These entries will be assigned to the variable as follows:

```
A$ = "JOHN"
B$ = "SMITH"
 C = 281
```

If an incorrect number of entries were made or if a string constant were input for a numeric variable or vice versa, the following message will be displayed,

> ? Redo from start
> ?

and the computer will wait for a valid entry.

It is good programming practice to include a prompt message with the INPUT statement to let the operator know what data the computer is expecting. For example, the following INPUT statement,

    100 INPUT "ENTER COMPANY NAME, NUMBER"; A$, B

would result in the following prompt being displayed:

    ENTER COMPANY NAME, NUMBER? <u>ACME MFG INC, 27</u>

These entries will be assigned to the variables A$ and B as follows:

    A$ = "ACME MFG INC"
    B = 27

Loops

Suppose that you needed to compute the squares of the integers from 1 to 20. One way of doing this is by calculating the square for each individual integer as shown below:

```
100  A = 1^2
200  PRINT A
300  B = 2 ^ 2
400  PRINT B
500  C = 3^2
600  PRINT C
       .
       .
       .
```

However, this method is very cumbersome. This problem could be solved much more efficiently through the use of a FOR, NEXT loop as shown below.

```
100  FOR A = 1 TO 20
200  X = A^2
300  PRINT X
400  NEXT A
500  END
```

The sequence of statements from 100 to 400 is known as a **loop.** When the computer encounters the FOR statement in line 100, the variable A is set to 1. X is then calculated and displayed in lines 200 and 300.

The NEXT statement in line 400 will request the next value for A. Execution returns to line 100 where the value of A is incremented by 1 (to 2) and then compared to the value appearing after TO. Since the value of A is less than that value, the loop will be executed again with the value of A set at 2.

The loop will continue to be executed until A attains a value greater than 20. When this occurs, the statement following the NEXT statement will be executed.

In our preceding example, A is known as an **index variable.** If the optional keyword STEP is not included with the FOR statement, the index variable will be incremented by 1 every time the NEXT statement is executed.

STEP can be included at the end of a FOR statement to change the value by which the index variable is incremented. The integer appearing after STEP is the new increment. For example, if our preceding example were changed as follows,

```
100  FOR A = 1 TO 20 STEP 2
200  X = A^2
300  PRINT X
400  NEXT A
500  END
```

the index variable A would be incremented by 2 every time the NEXT statement was executed.

Conditional Statements

One of the most important features of a computer is its ability to make a decision. BASIC uses the IF, THEN, ELSE statement to take advantage of the computer's decision making ability. The IF, THEN, ELSE statement takes the following form:

IF *expression* THEN *statement* ELSE *statement*

The IF statement sets up a question or a condition. If the answer to that question is true, the *statement* following THEN is executed. If the answer is false, the *statement* following ELSE will be executed.

In the following example, if X is equal to 1, then Y will be set to 1. If X is not equal to 1, Y will be set to 0:

100 IF X = 1 THEN Y = 1 ELSE Y = 0

The IF, THEN, ELSE statement may be shortened to just IF, THEN as shown below:

100 Y = 0
200 IF X = 1 THEN Y = 1

In this example, if X is equal to 1, the statement following THEN will be executed. If X is not equal to 1, program execution will continue with the next program statement (in our example--line 200).

Branching Statements

Branching statements change the execution pattern of programs from their usual line by line execution in ascending line number order. A branching statement allows program control to be altered to any line number desired. The most commonly used branching statements in BASIC are GOTO and GOSUB. We will discuss GOTO here. GOSUB will be covered in the next Chapter in the section covering subroutines.

GOTO takes the following format:

GOTO *line number*

For example, the following program statement:

```
500  GOTO 999
     .
     .
999  END
```

would branch program control at line 500 to line 999.

Branching statements are often used in conjunction with conditional statements. In such a situation, the normal execution of the program is altered depending upon the outcome of the condition set up in the IF statement. This is shown in the following example:

```
100  INPUT "ENTER THE AMOUNT"; A
200  IF A = 0 THEN GOTO 900
     .
     .
900  PRINT "ARE YOU FINISHED (Y/N)"; A$
910  IF A$ = 'N' THEN GOTO 100
920  IF A$ = 'Y' THEN 999 ELSE 900
999  END
```

In our preceding example, if the value input for A has a zero value, then the program will branch to line 900 where the operator will be prompted whether he has finished entering data. In line 910, the program will set up a condition where if the input was 'N', the program will branch to line 100. If the entry was not equal to 'N', the program will continue to line 920.

In line 920, the program will check to see if the value input was equal to 'Y'. If so, the program will branch to line 999 where it will end. If not, the program will branch to line 900 where the operator will be prompted again for an entry of 'Y' or 'N'.

Note in line 920 that a GOTO statement is not used to precede the line number being branched to. When a line number is indicated following a THEN or ELSE statement, the computer does not require the presence of GOTO, which is assumed.

CHAPTER 4.
MORE IBM BASIC CONCEPTS

Introduction

In this chapter, we will continue our discussion of programming in IBM BASIC. We will introduce additional, more advanced features of IBM BASIC. These include the following:

>Tables and Arrays
>Subroutines and GOSUB
>Advanced Printing Concepts
>Random Number Generation
>String Handling
>Conversion of Numeric Types
>Functions and DEF FN
>Graphics

An understanding of these concepts will help you become more skillful and proficient in the use of IBM BASIC.

Tables & Arrays

In Chapter 2, we introduced the concept of variables. A variable is designed to hold a single data item--either string or numeric. However, some programs require that thousands or even hundreds of thousands of variable names be used.

Obviously, the use of thousands of individual variable names could prove extremely cumbersome. To solve this problem, BASIC allows the use of **subscripted variables.** Subscripted variables are identified with a **subscript,** a number appearing within parentheses immediately after the variable name. An example of a group of subscripted variables is given below:

$$A(0),\ A(1),\ A(2),\ A(3),\ A(4),...,\ A(100)$$

Note that each subscripted variable is a unique variable. In other words, A(0) differs from A(1), A(2), A(3), A(4), etc.

Subscripted variables should be visualized as an array (or table). In our previous example, the data contained in the array defined by A would consist of one row with 101 columns in it. Such an array is a single-dimension array.

An array can also consist of two dimensions. Such an array is known as a two-dimensional array (or table). An example of an array of 4 rows and 3 columns is shown in Illustration 4-1.

A two-dimensional array contains two subscripts. The first subscript contains the row location, while the second subscript contains the column location. The subscripted variable A(1,0) identifies the darkened area in the array shown in Illustration 4-1.

Illustration 4-1. Two-Dimensional Array

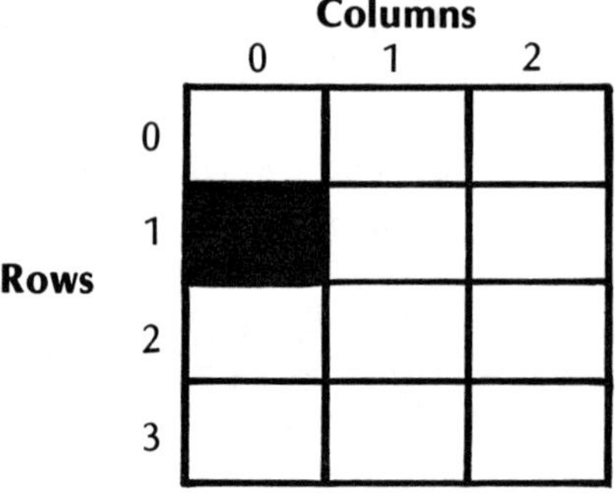

Arrays can be used with string as well as numeric data. Illustration 4-2 depicts a two-dimensional array containing string data. In our example, location A$(5,0) would contain the string "KELLY".

Before an array variable can be used in a program, the size of that array must have been defined so that BASIC can reserve a memory area for it. This is accomplished with the DIM (for dimension) statement. A single dimension numeric array with 101 variables could be defined with the following DIM statement:

DIM A(100)

The two-dimensional string array shown in Illustration 4-2 could be dimensioned with the following DIM statement:

DIM A$(5,2)

Illustration 4-2. Two-Dimensional Array (String Data)

	0	1	2
0	DOE	JOHN	278-78-4321
1	EAST	BYRON	239-49-2038
2	FLINT	JOHN	264-44-2279
3	HARRIS	BILL	289-23-3299
4	JOHNSON	JACK	282-28-4211
5	KELLY	TED	278-48-2811

A$

More than one array can be defined with a single DIM statement as shown in the example below:

100 DIM A$(5,2), A(100), B(2,3)

If an array variable is encountered before that array has been dimensioned with a DIM statement, BASIC will assume that the array is single dimensional with subscripts ranging from 0 to 10.

Using an array variable before it has been dimensioned can be the source of a potential error. If BASIC encounters a DIM statement after an array has been previously dimensioned, the following error message will be displayed:

Duplicate Definition

Therefore, if an array variable is encountered that had not been dimensioned, that array would be dimensioned by default. If that array is subsequently dimensioned again with a DIM statement, a Duplicate Definition error will occur.

DATA & READ Statements

In Chapter 3, we discussed how data could be assigned to a variable with a LET statement as well as how data could be input directly from the keyboard and assigned to a variable with the INPUT statement.

However, neither the LET nor the INPUT statements are practical for assigning data values to the individual variables in a large table. DATA and READ statements are much more practical for assigning values to variables in an array. DATA and READ statements can be used for assigning values to any variable--not just array variables.

A typical DATA statement is shown below:

    100 DATA "WILLIAMS", 27, "ST. LOUIS", "314-727-1141"

Notice that this DATA statement contains four data items, three of which are string and one which is numeric. In our example, we have enclosed the string data items in quotation marks. However, this was not actually required. In a DATA statement, a string only needs to be enclosed in quotation marks if it contains a comma, a colon, or if its first character is a blank space.

DATA statements are used in tandem with READ statements to assign data values to variables. An example of a READ statement is given below:

    200 READ NAME$, AGE, CITY$, PHONE$

When a READ statement is executed, the computer will first search for a DATA statement. When a DATA statement is found, the values in the DATA statement will be assigned one-by-one to the variables in the READ statement.

If the first DATA statement encountered does not have enough data items to be assigned to all the variables in the READ statement, the next DATA statement will be searched for. The values from this and succeeding DATA statements will continue to be assigned to the variables in the READ statement until all of the variables in the READ statement have been assigned a value.

The computer keeps track of the next DATA statement data item to be used via an internal pointer. When any future READ statements are executed, this pointer will determine which is the next data item to be read into the READ statement variable.

BASIC includes a statement known as RESTORE, which when executed, sets the DATA item pointer back to the beginning of the DATA statement list. The use of the DATA item pointer and the effect of RESTORE on it is depicted in Illustration 4-3.

Illustration 4-3. DATA Statement Pointer

```
100  DATA 537, 27, WILSON, 276-46-4142
200  READ A, B
300  READ C$, D$
```

DATA Item List

| 537 | 27 | WILSON | 276-46-4142 |

Data Statement Pointer (Before Line 200)   Data Statement Pointer (After Line 200)   Data Statement Pointer (After Line 300)

```
400  RESTORE
500  READ X, Y, Z$
```

DATA Item List

| 537 | 27 | WILSON | 276-46-4142 |

Data Statement Pointer (After Line 400)   Data Statement Pointer (After Line 500)

When not used properly, DATA and READ statements can be the source of program errors. One potential error source occurs when the program attempts to READ more data items than were given in the DATA statements. Such an error would occur in the following program:

```
100 DATA 7, 8, 11, 13, 15
200 FOR I = 1 TO 7
300 READ X(I)
400 PRINT X(I)
500 NEXT
600 END
```

In the preceding example, the program would attempt to read 7 data items. However, since the DATA statement only contained 5 data items, the following error message would appear:

```
Out of data in 300
```

Another potential source of an error when executing DATA and READ statements are situations where the program attempts to read a numeric data item into a string variable or vice versa. If such an error is encountered, the following error message will be displayed:

```
Type mismatch
```

DATA and READ statements often are used in conjunction with FOR, NEXT loops to read large amounts of data into arrays. An example of this use of FOR, NEXT is given below:

```
100 DATA 100, 200, 300, 400
200 DATA 500, 600, 700, 800
300 DATA 900, 1000, 1100, 1200
400 DIM A(3,4)
500 FOR I = 1 TO 3
600 FOR J = 1 TO 4
700 READ A(I,J)
800 NEXT
900 NEXT
      .
      .
      .
```

The preceding program would read data items into array A( ) as shown in Illustration 4-4.

Illustration 4-4. A ( ) Array Values

	0	1	2	3	4
0					
1		100	200	300	400
2		500	600	700	800
3		900	1000	1100	1200

Subroutines & GOSUB

Many times you will find that the same set of program instructions are used more than once in a program. Re-entering these instructions throughout the program can be very time consuming. By using **subroutines,** these additional entries will be unnecessary.

A subroutine can be defined as a program which appears within another larger program. The subroutine may be executed as many times as desired.

The execution of subroutines is controlled by the GOSUB and RETURN statements. The format for the GOSUB statement is as follows:

GOSUB *line number*

The computer will begin execution of the subroutine beginning at the *line number* indicated. Statements will continue to be executed in order, until a RETURN statement is encountered. Upon execution of the RETURN statement, the computer will branch out of the subroutine back to the first line following the original GOSUB statement. This is illustrated in the following example.

Illustration 4-5. BASIC Program With A Subroutine

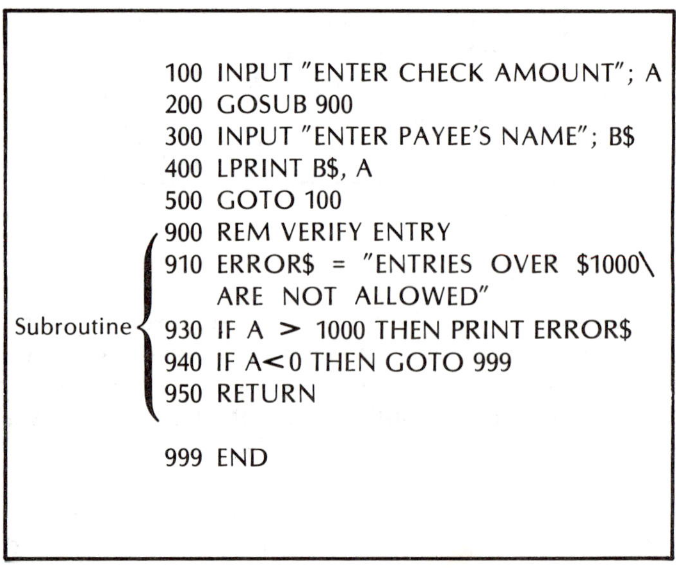

Subroutines can help the programmer organize his program more efficiently. Subroutines also can make writing a program easier. By dividing a lengthy program into a number of smaller subroutines, the complexity of the program will be reduced. Individual subroutines are smaller and, therefore, more easily written. Subroutines are also more easily debugged than a longer program.

Advanced Printing

In Chapter 3, we introduced the concept of outputting data to the screen or printer with the PRINT and LPRINT statements. In this chapter, we will expand upon this concept.

In Chapter 3, we learned that placing a comma between data items that are to be printed results in each data item being printed at the beginning of a print zone. If you wish data items printed next to each other with no spaces in between, you can do so by using a semicolon (;) to separate the data items.

For example, the following series of program statements,

```
100  A = -7
200  LPRINT "THE ANSWER IS ";A
300  END
```

results in the following being ouput by the printer:

```
THE ANSWER IS -7
```

Note that the string in the LPRINT statement contains a blank space as its last character so that a space exists between IS and -7 in the printer output. If A were a positive value, the blank space in the string would not be necessary. This is because BASIC automatically prints a blank space in front of all positive numbers. This blank space replaces the plus (+) sign.

For example, this series of program statements,

```
100  A = 7
200  LPRINT "THE ANSWER IS"; A
300  END
```

would result in the following printer output:

```
THE ANSWER IS 7
```

BASIC allows an item to be printed in any position on the screen or printer with the TAB command. The print position can range from 1 to 255 from left to right. The TAB statement allows the user to move to any one of these positions. For example, the following statement,

```
100  PRINT TAB(10) X; TAB(15) Y
```

will print the numeric data in X at print position 10 and the data in Y at print position 15. Notice that a semicolon is used to separate the two TAB statements.

In the preceding paragraph, we mentioned that print positions can range from 1 to 255. These 255 print positions are the result of the fact that a logical line in IBM BASIC can consist of up to 255 characters. The IBM video display can be either set for 40 characters per line or 80 characters per line (with the WIDTH statement as discussed later).

If a line being sent to the video display consists of a greater number of characters than the width of the screen, the extra characters will 'wrap around' to the next line. Likewise, if a line being output to the printer contains a greater number of characters than allowed for, the excess characters will be printed on successive lines.

Formatting Characters

BASIC allows the user to format numeric data when it is output to the screen or to the printer. Formatting is accomplished through the use of the PRINT USING statement and a **format string.** The format string contains the formatting characters enclosed in quotation marks which determines the appearance of the numeric data when it is output.

The following statement,

```
100  PRINT USING "#####.##";X
```

will result in the numeric value in variable X being output in decimal form with five digits to the right of the decimal point, and two digits to the left. The # in the format string is used to represent a digit while the period is used to represent a decimal point.

If the following numeric data items were printed with the preceding statement's format string,

```
        7
 18971.17
    18.5782
   999.77
 10000.01
985712.11
```

The following would be output:

```
     7.00
 18971.17
    18.57
   999.77
 10000.01
%985712.11
```

Note that the final data item has a value greater than that allowed for by the format string. In these situations, the number will be displayed with a leading percent character (%).

A second formatting character, the dollar sign ($), is often used with the digit character (#) to display monetary figures. A single dollar sign in a format string causes the $ to be printed in that position in the output. If we assume the value of X to be 17.98, the following statement,

```
100  PRINT USING "$####.##";A
```

would result in the following output:

```
$  17.98
```

The inclusion of two dollar signs ($$) in the format string is known as the floating dollar sign. The floating dollar sign results in a single dollar sign character being printed to the immediate left of the numeric value being output. Again, if we assume the value of X to be 17.98, the following statement,

```
100  PRINT USING "$$####.##";A
```

would result in the following output:

```
$17.98
```

The format string can also be used to include commas when printing large numbers. If we assume the value of A to be 999999, the following statement,

```
100  PRINT USING "###,###.##";A
```

would result in the following output:

```
999,999.00
```

The format string can also be used to include a numeric value's sign in its output. By including the addition sign (+) at the beginning or end of the format string, the number's sign (+ or –) will be printed in the position specified. For example, if we assume the value of A to be –77.1, the following statement,

```
100  PRINT USING "+###.##";A
```

would result in the following output:

```
– 77.1
```

The output could be altered by using the following format string:

```
100  PRINT USING "###.##+";A
```

```
77.1–
```

Another formatting character, leading asterisks (**), will cause all blank digit positions in a format string to be filled with asterisks. If we assume that A has a value of 58.29, the following statement:

100 PRINT USING "**####.##";A

would result in the following output:

**58.29

Another formatting character, the trailing minus sign (–), causes the number to be output with a trailing minus sign if that number has a negative value and no sign if it is positive. If we assume A's value to be –79, the following statement,

100 PRINT USING "####-";A

would output the following:

79–

Again, in this section, we have used the PRINT and PRINT USING statements in our examples to send output to the screen. That output could just as easily have been sent to the printer by using the LPRINT and LPRINT USING statements.

Line Width

IBM BASIC'S WIDTH command allows the user to change the line width of the video display or printer.

The video display's width can be set to either 40 or 80 characters. If your video screen's width is set to 80 (automatic with monochrome monitor display), the width can be changed to 40 with the following statement:

100 WIDTH 40

The display will then include only 40 characters in each line. However, each character will be twice as wide as characters displayed in an 80 character line width. The following statement can be used to return to an 80 character width:

100 WIDTH 80

The LPRINT and LPRINT USING statements assume a printer width of 80 characters. However, this width can be changed by executing a WIDTH "LPT 1:" statement as shown below:

100 WIDTH "LPT 1:" 131

LPT 1: is the device name for the printer.

Random Number Generator

IBM BASIC includes features which allow the user to generate random numbers. This is accomplished with the BASIC function RND. RND generates a random number that lies between 0.000000 and 1.000000. Every time the RND function is called, the computer chooses at random a number from within this range.

In the following statement, the random number generated is assigned to the numeric variable A:

100 A = RND

Random numbers generated by RND are based upon a random number **seed.** The seed controls the series of random numbers generated by the computer. Therefore, to get a truly random series of numbers, the user must periodically change the seed.

The random number seed is changed with the RANDOMIZE command. When RANDOMIZE is used without a parameter, as shown below,

100 RANDOMIZE

the following message will be displayed:

Random seed number (–32768 to 32767)?

The user must then enter the desired seed within this range. RND will then generate random numbers based upon the seed entered.

The RANDOMIZE statement can also assume the following form:

100 RANDOMIZE 1478

When the preceding command is executed, no user prompt will be displayed. The seed will automatically be set to 1478.

String Handling

As a programmer, you will encounter a number of situations where you may need to work with string data. For example, you might want to combine several strings, compare two strings, separate portions of a string, or even convert string data to its numeric equivalent. IBM BASIC allows for all of these.

String Concatenation

The process of joining together one or more strings is known as **concatenation.**The arithmetic operator for addition (+) is used for string concatenation. However, concatenation is very different from addition. In concatenation, the strings being concatenated are joined to form a new string as shown below:

```
Ok
100  A$ = "JOHN"
200  B$ = "SON"
300  C$ = A$ + B$
400  PRINT C$
500  END
RUN
  JOHNSON
Ok
```

Either string constants or variables may be concatenated. Any number of strings may be concatenated as long as the resulting string contains 255 or fewer characters.

Comparing Strings

The same relational operators are used for comparing strings as are used for comparing numeric data. These include the following:

$$< \quad \text{or LT} \longrightarrow \text{less than}$$
$$<= \quad \text{or LE} \longrightarrow \text{less than or equal to}$$
$$> \quad \text{or GT} \longrightarrow \text{greater than}$$
$$>= \quad \text{or GE} \longrightarrow \text{greater than or equal to}$$
$$= \quad \text{or EQ} \longrightarrow \text{equal to}$$
$$<> \quad \text{or NE} \longrightarrow \text{not equal}$$

Strings are compared one character at a time beginning with each string's first character. This comparison is made with each character's corresponding ASCII code.

Fortunately, ASCII code comparisons are relatively simple. A comparison of the characters by ASCII codes is almost identical to an alphabetical comparison. A character is less than another with respect to ASCII codes, if that character precedes it in the alphabet. Lowercase letters are always greater than their uppercase counterparts and numbers are always less than letters. Appendix A contains the ASCII character codes.

If two strings with differing lengths are being compared, the longer string is always evaluated as being the greater. In other words, "aaaa" is greater than "aaa".

Like numeric relational operators, string relational operators return a value of 0 if the relation is false and a value of –1 if it is true. Whenever strings are being compared, they must be enclosed within quotation marks.

String Handling Functions

IBM BASIC contains a number of string handling functions which allow the user to extract a part of a string or to replace a part of a string with a different string. These functions are LEFT$, MID$, RIGHT$, LEN, and MATCH.

The LEFT$ function takes the following format,

$$LEFT\$ \ (string,X)$$

where *string* is the string from which characters are to be extracted and *X* is the number of characters to be extracted. The LEFT$ function will extract the leftmost number of characters given in *X* from the string given in *string*.

Illustration 4-6 contains an example of the use of LEFT$.

Illustration 4-6. LEFT$

```
Ok
100  A$ = "JOHNSON"
200  B$ = LEFT$(A$,4)
300  PRINT B$
400  END
RUN
  JOHN
Ok
```

The RIGHT$ function functions exactly like the LEFT$ function except that the rightmost number of characters specified are returned. Illustration 4-7 contains an example of the use of RIGHT$.

Illustration 4-7. RIGHT$

```
Ok
100  A$ = "JOHNSON"
200  B$ = RIGHT$(A$,3)
300  PRINT B$
400  END
RUN
   SON
Ok
```

The MID$ function can be used to either return a portion of a string or to replace a portion of one string with another string. MID$ takes the following format when used to return a portion of a string:

$$a\$ = MID\$ \ (b\$, \ x[,y])$$

The string being returned is $a\$$. $a\$$ is being returned from $b\$$. The string being returned will begin with the x character in $b\$$. The number of characters returned from $b\$$ is specified in y. y is an optional parameter. If y is omitted, all rightmost characters in $b\$$ will be returned in $a\$$. An example of the use of MID$ to return a portion of a string is given in Illustration 4-8.

Illustration 4-8. MID$ Used To Return A Portion Of A String

```
Ok
100  X$ = "NEW CASTLE"
200  Y$ = MID$(X$,5,4)
300  PRINT Y$
400  END
RUN
  CAST
Ok
```

To replace a portion of a given string with another string, use the format given below:

$$MID\$\ (b\$,\ x[,y]) = a\$$$

The string given in a$ will replace the characters in b$ beginning at the xth character in b$. y is an optional parameter which indicates the number of characters from a$ which will be used in the replacement. An example of the use of MID$ to replace a portion of a string is given in Illustraion 4-9.

Illustration 4-9. MID\$ Used To Replace A Portion Of A String

```
Ok
100  X$ = "NEW CASTLE":Y$ = "MUNSON"
200  MID$ (X$,5) = Y$
300  PRINT X$
400  END
RUN
   NEW MUNSON
Ok
```

String/Numeric Data Conversion

Programmers often encounter situations where numeric data must be converted into string data and vice versa. This is often the case where a function is being used which will accept only string or numeric data as its arguments.

The STR\$ and VAL functions are used to convert numeric data to its string equivalent and strings to their numeric equivalent respectively. The ASC function is used to convert a single text character to its ASCII numeric equivalent. The CHR\$ function converts an ASCII numeric code to an equivalent text character.

Examples of the use of STR\$, VAL, CHR\$, and ASC are given in Illustration 4-10 and 4-11.

Illustration 4-10. STR$ And VAL Examples

```
Ok
100  ZIP = 33578
200  ZIP$ = STR$(ZIP)           REM ZIP$ = "33578"
300  ZIP2 = 33579
400  ZIP2$ = STR$(ZIP2)
500  ZIP3$ = ZIP$ + ZIP2$       REM  ZIP3$ = "3357833579"
600  ZIP3 = VAL(ZIP3$)          REM  ZIP3 = 3357833579
700  ZIP4 = INT(ZIP3/10000)
800  PRINT ZIP4
900  END
RUN
  335783
Ok
```

Illustration 4-11. CHR$ And ASC Examples

```
Ok
100  A$ = "GILBERT"
200  A1% = ASC(A$)
300  PRINT A1%
400  X% = 90
500  X$ = CHR$(X%)
600  PRINT X$
700  END
RUN
  71
  Z
Ok
```

Mathematical Functions

IBM BASIC contains a number of built-in functions. These are described individually in detail in Chapter 7. The majority of the IBM BASIC functions are used in mathematical applications. The availability of these built-in mathematical functions allows for more efficient programs involving mathematical calculations.

All of the IBM BASIC mathematical functions operate in much the same manner. Each function is defined by a reserved word (ex. SIN for Sine, COS for Cosine, LOG for Logarithm, etc.).

A numeric constant, variable, or expression will appear in parentheses following the reserved word which identifies the function. The function for that numeric value will then be calculated by the computer. The use of several mathematical functions is shown in Illustration 4-12.

IBM BASIC includes the following three trigonometric functions:

       SIN(N) = sine of the angle given in N.
       COS(N) = cosine of the angle given in N.
       TAN(N) = tangent of the angle given in N.

The angle N must be given in terms of radians. One radian is the equivalent of 57.29578 degrees. One degree equals .017453 radians.

Therefore, the following can be used to calculate a trigonometric function with its argument (X) given in degrees:

       SIN(.017453*X)
       COS(.017453*X)
       TAN(.017453*X)

The other three trigonometric functions, secant, cosecant, and cotangent can be computed by using SIN, COS, and TAN as shown in the following formulas:

       SEC(X) = 1/COS(X)
       CSC(X) = 1/SIN(X)
       COT(X) = COS(X)/SIN(X)

Illustration 4-12. Mathematical Functions

```
Ok
 100  PRINT SIN(.47)
 200  PRINT COS(.98)
 300  PRINT TAN(.37)
 400  PRINT SQR(49)
 500  PRINT INT(5.79)
 600  PRINT INT(-5.79)
 700  PRINT FIX(7.93)
 800  PRINT FIX(-7.93)
 900  PRINT ABS(-4.7)
1000  PRINT SGN(2.7)
1100  PRINT SGN(-2.7)
1200  END
  .4528862
  .5570225
  .3878631
  7
  5
 -6
  7
 -7
  4.7
 +1
 -1
```

IBM BASIC also includes the arctangent function ATN. This function returns the angle (expressed in radians) whose tangent is given in its argument.

$$ATN(X) = \text{angle in radians whose tangent equals X.}$$

The following formula can be used to calculate the angle expressed in degrees (rather than radians) whose tangent is given in X.

$$57.29578 * ATN(X)$$

IBM BASIC also contains functions for calculating logarithms and exponents. The exponential function takes the following form:

$$A = EXP(B)$$

The preceding EXP function is calculated by computing the value of e raised to the B power. e is known as the base of natural logarithms. The value of e in IBM BASIC is 2.71828183.

The natural logarithm of a number may be calculated with the LOG function.

$$LOG(X) = \text{natural logarithm of X.}$$

Logarithms with a base other than 10 may be calculated using the following formula,

$$LOG_b(X) = LOG(X)/LOG(b)$$

where b is the base of the logarithm.

IBM BASIC includes the SQR function for determining the square root of its argument.

$$SQR(X) = \text{square root of X.}$$

The square root of a number can also be calculated with the exponential arithmetic operator. The following expression,

$$X^{\wedge}(1/2)$$

will calculate the square root of X. The exponential arithmetic operator can also be used to calculate a root other than the square root (ex. cube root), as shown below:

$$X^{\wedge}(1/3)$$

IBM BASIC also includes several functions that can be used in working with numeric values. These include INT, FIX, ABS, SGN, CINT, CSNG, and CDBL.

The INT function returns the integer with the greatest value which is less than or equal to its argument. INT takes the following form:

INT(X) = highest integer whose value is less than or equal to X.

Illustration 4-12 contains examples of the usage of the INT function.

The FIX function is used to discard the decimal portion of a numeric value. FIX takes the following form:

FIX(X) = integer portion of X.

Illustration 4-12 contains examples of the usage of the FIX function.

The ABS function returns the absolute value of its argument. ABS takes the following form:

$$ABS(X) = |x|$$

An example of the use of ABS appears in Illustration 4-12.

The SGN function returns the sign of its argument. An example of the use of SGN appears in Illustration 4-12.

The CINT function is used to convert its argument to an integer. The decimal portion of the argument will be truncated. CINT can only be used with numbers in the range between –32768 and 32767.

The CSGN function is used to convert its argument to a **single-precision number.** A single-precision number is one that contains seven or fewer digits.

The CDBL function is used to convert its argument to a **double-precision number.** A double-precision number is one that contains over seven digits.

User-Defined Functions

In the preceding section, we discussed a number of predefined IBM BASIC functions. IBM BASIC also allows the user to define his own functions. These are known as **user-defined** functions. A user-defined function must be defined with the DEF FN statement before it can be used in the program.

For example, the following DEF FN statement would define a function in which the argument was squared and 1 was then subtracted from the product:

$$100 \ \ DEF \ FNA(X) = X \wedge 2 - 1$$

Notice that the letter A was used to identify the function. FNA( ) may be used throughout the program to calculate the square of its argument less 1. Obviously, if the calculation defined by a function is performed over and over in a program, the use of a user-defined function can save a great deal of re-entry of the necessary program lines.

Any valid variable name may be used as a user-defined function name. The following would be a valid function name:

$$FNHEX.TO.DEC\%$$

A function may be used in the definition of another function--as long as that function has already been defined.

Finally, a function may be used to produce a string. Such a function's name must end with the dollar sign ($) as shown in the example below:

$$DEF \ FNA\$(X\$,N) = RIGHT\$(X\$,N)$$

Graphics

Graphics can be used with IBM BASIC to output pictures, graphs, or charts. Graphics can be used in either of the three IBM PC display modes; **text, medium resolution graphics,** and **high resolution graphics.**

The text mode can be used to display characters on the video screen. These include the ASCII characters (ex. letters, number, etc.) as well as the graphics characters.

The medium resolution graphics mode allows the user to draw pictures in color or in black and white. The color/graphics interface must be present if the medium resolution graphics mode is to be used.

The high resolution mode allows the user to output more detailed figures. However, these can only be output in black and white — not in color.

The mode desired by the user can be specified with the SCREEN statement as follows:

```
SCREEN 0 = text mode
SCREEN 1 = medium resolution graphics mode
SCREEN 2 = high resolution graphics mode
```

Upon BASIC start-up, the display is automatically in the text mode. Subsequent SCREEN statements can be used to change modes.

Text Mode

In the text mode, the IBM PC display screen is divided into 25 rows of either 40 or 80 characters each. This gives a total of 2000 possible character positions.

A specific screen position can be identified with the LOCATE statement. LOCATE moves the cursor to the position indicated. LOCATE takes the following form,

```
LOCATE x,y
```

where x identifies the row and y identifies the column. For example, the following statements,

```
100  LOCATE 15,30
200  PRINT CHR$(198)
```

would position the cursor at row 15 and column 30 on the screen and print the graphics character ⊨ at that position.

Medium Resolution Graphics Mode

In the medium resolution graphics mode, the screen is divided into 320 positions horizontally and 200 positions vertically. Each of the 641,000 small rectangles created by this division of the screen is known as a **pixel** (for picture element). Each pixel is an independent entity and can be turned on or off or assigned any color as specified by the user.

Medium resolution graphics is selected with one of the following statements:

100 SCREEN 1,0
or
100 SCREEN 1,1

The first statement enables the color graphics feature, while the second disables the color graphics feature.

Pixels, like character positions in the text mode, are identified with a pair of x,y coordinates where x indicates the row number and y the column. The rows are numbered from 0 to 199 and the columns from 0 to 319.

In medium resolution graphics, the COLOR statement may be used to select any of the following 16 background colors. These are as follows:

0 = black	8 = grey
1 = blue	9 = light blue
2 = green	10 = light green
3 = cyan	11 = light cyan
4 = red	12 = light red
5 = magenta	13 = light magenta
6 = brown	14 = yellow
7 = white	15 = high intensity white

The foreground colors in medium resolution graphics are selected from one of the following two palettes:

	Palette 0	Palette 1
	1 = green	1 = cyan
	2 = red	2 = magenta
	3 = brown	3 = white

The background color and foreground palette are selected with the COLOR statement:

100 COLOR 10,1

The preceding example sets the background color to 10 (light green) and the palette as 1. A different background color and/or palette can be chosen with a new COLOR statement.

The PSET and LINE statements can be used to draw color graphics figures. An example of the PSET statement is given below:

200 PSET (200,150), 2

The preceding statement will turn on the pixel at column 200 and row 150 in color 2 of the previously set palette (1). This color would be magenta. The PRESET statement can be used to turn off a pixel. The following PRESET statement turns off the preceding PSET statement.

300 PRESET (200, 150)

PSET and PRESET statements can specify a pixel location in relative form through the use of the optional STEP statement. For example in the following statement,

400 PSET STEP (–50,50), 1

color 1 will be turned on at the pixel which is located 50 locations to the left and 50 rows down from the current cursor location (200, 150 in line 300).

In the medium and high resolution graphics modes, the LINE statement can be used to draw lines and even rectangles in the screen. The following LINE statement,

```
100  LINE (10,20) – (70,100)
```

would draw a line from location (10,20) to location (70,100). The LINE statement could be used in the following form to draw a line from the current cursor position to location (80,200):

```
200  LINE - (80,200)
```

The STEP statement can be used to specify relative positions in a LINE statement just as in the PSET and PRESET statements. The following statement,

```
300  LINE - STEP(50, –100)
```

would cause a line to be drawn from the current cursor position to the pixel which is 50 positions to the right and 100 rows above the current cursor position.

The LINE statement can also be used to specify the color of the line being drawn. In the following statement,

```
400  LINE(70,70) - (100,100), 2
```

color 2 of the current palette would be used.

The LINE statement can also be used to draw a rectangle by using the B (for Box) parameter. The following statement,

```
500  LINE (200,200) - (300,300), 1, B
```

would draw a rectangle with opposite corners located at pixel (200,200) and pixel (300,300). The outline of the box would be in color 1 of the current palette. The inside of the rectangle can be filled with the same color as its edges by using BF (box filled) rather than B.

Logical Operators

Logical or Boolean operators are generally used in IBM BASIC to compare the outcomes of two relational operations. Logical operations themselves return a true or false value which will be used to determine program flow.

The logical operators are NOT (logical complement), AND (conjunction), OR (disjunction), XOR (exclusive or), IMP (implication), and EQV (equivalence). These return results as shown in Illustration 4-13.

A logical operator evaluates an input of one or more operands with true or false values. The logical operator evaluates these true or false values and returns a value of true or false itself. An operand of a logical operator is evaluated as true if it has a non-zero value. (Remember, relational operators return a value of -1 for a true value.) An operand of a logical operator is evaluated as false if it is equal to zero.

The result of a logical operation is also a number which, if non-zero, is considered true, and false if it is true.

The following are examples of the use of logical operators in combination with relational operators in decision-making:

```
IF X>10 OR Y<0 THEN 900
IF A>0 AND B>0 THEN 200 ELSE GOTO 300
ERROR.FLAG% = NOT ERROR.FLAG%
```

In the first example, the result of the logical operation will be true if variable X has a value greater than 10 or if variable Y has a value less than 0. Otherwise, it will be false. If the result of the logical operation is true, the program will branch to line 900. Otherwise, it will continue to the next statement.

In the second example, the result of the logical operation will be true only if the value of both variables A and B are greater than zero. If the result of the logical operation is true, program control will branch to line 200. Otherwise, program control will branch to line 300.

In the final example, the value of ERROR.FLAG% is switched from true to false or vice versa.

Illustration 4-13 contains tables that may prove helpful when evaluating program statements using logical operators in combination with relational operators.

Illustration 4-13. Logical Operators

NOT Operation

T	F

A Operand

F	T

NOT A

OR Operation

T	T	F	F

A Operand

T	F	T	F

B Operand

T	T	T	F

A OR B

AND Operation

T	T	F	F

A Operand

T	F	T	F

B Operand

T	F	F	F

A AND B

XOR Operation

T	T	F	F	A Operand
T	F	T	F	B Operand
F	T	T	F	A XOR B

IMP Operation

T	T	F	F	A Operand
T	F	T	F	B Operand
T	F	T	T	A IMP B

EQV Operation

T	T	F	F	A Operand
T	F	T	F	B Operand
T	F	F	T	A EQV B

Logical operands actually convert their operands to their 16 bit binary equivalents before evaluating them. If an operand is negative, the two's complement is used to form that operand's 16-bit equivalent.

Illustration 4-14 gives examples of the conversion of decimal integers to their 16-bit equivalent.

Illustration 4-14. Converting Integers To Their 16-Bit Equivalents

Positive Integers--Decimal To Binary

$$87_{10} = 0\ 1\ 0\ 1\ 0\ 1\ 1\ 1_2$$
$$16_{10} = 0\ 0\ 0\ 1\ 0\ 0\ 0\ 0_2$$
$$33_{10} = 0\ 0\ 1\ 0\ 0\ 0\ 0\ 1_2$$

Negative Integers--Two's Complement

-87_{10}

Step 1. Calculate 87_{10} in binary	0 1 0 1 0 1 1 1
Step 2. Calculate NOT(01010111)	1 0 1 0 1 0 0 0
Step 3. Add 1 For Final Result	1 0 1 0 1 0 0 1

-16_{10}

Step 1. Calculate 16_{10} in binary	0 0 0 1 0 0 0 0
Step 2. Calculate NOT(00010000)	1 1 1 0 1 1 1 1
Step 3. Add 1 For Final Result	1 1 1 1 0 0 0 0

-33_{10}

Step 1. Calculate 33_{10} in binary	0 0 1 0 0 0 0 1
Step 2. Calculate NOT(00100001)	1 1 0 1 1 1 1 0
Step 3. Add 1 For Final Result	1 1 0 1 1 1 1 1

The following example illustrates the use of the logical operators with positive and negative integers.

Z = 27 AND 9

0	0	0	1	1	0	1	1	Operand 1 = 27_{10}
0	0	0	0	1	0	0	1	Operand 2 = 9_{10}
0	0	0	0	1	0	0	1	Z = 27_{10} AND 9_{10}

$$Z = 9_{10}$$

Z = 24 OR –7

0	0	0	1	1	0	0	0	Operand 1 = 24_{10}
1	1	1	1	1	0	0	1	Operand 2 = -7_{10}
1	1	1	1	1	0	0	1	Z = 24_{10} OR -7_{10}

$$Z = 249_{10}$$

Z = 9 XOR 33

128	64	32	16	8	4	2	1	
0	0	0	0	1	0	0	1	Operand 1 = 9_{10}
0	0	1	0	0	0	0	1	Operand 2 = 33_{10}
0	0	1	0	1	0	0	0	Z = 9_{10} XOR 33_{10}

$$Z = 40_{10}$$

Order Of Evaluation

In Chapter 3, we outlined the order of evaluation within an expression with respect to arithmetic and relational operators. Now that we have introduced the concepts of functions and logical operations, we can revise our order of evaluation as follows:

1. Function Calls

2. Arithmetic Operators
    a. Exponentiation $A \wedge B$
    b. Multiplication, Division $A*B$
                                            A/B
    c. Addition and Subtraction $A + B$
                                            $A - B$

3. Relational Operators
    a. Equality $A = B$
    b. Inequality $A<>B,\ A><B$
    c. Less Than $A<B$
    d. Greater Than $A>B$
    e. Less Than or Equal To $A<= B,\ A =<B$
    f. Greater Than or Equal To $A>= B,\ A =>B$

4. Logical Operators
    a. NOT
    b. AND
    c. OR
    d. XOR
    e. IMP
    f. EQV

CHAPTER 5.
FILES & FILE HANDLING WITH IBM BASIC

Introduction

In the preceding chapters, we did not discuss the concepts and programming techniques related to storage of data on cassette tape or floppy diskettes. In this chapter, we will discuss the concepts relating to the operation of the cassette tape device and diskette drives. We also will discuss how to write programs that make use of these devices.

Files, Records, & Fields

Before learning specific concepts relating to the cassette tape unit and diskette drives, it is essential that the user understand the concepts of **files, records,** and **fields.**

A file can be defined as a collection of related data. Files can be distinguished as being either **program files** or **data files.** A program file consists of a program which has been saved on diskette or cassette tape.

A data file consists of a collection of related information which has been saved on a diskette or cassette tape. Generally, a data file is to be read from storage by a program or written to storage by a program.

Data files are divided into smaller segments known as records and fields. A field is a single piece of data. Fields which are related are grouped together as a record. These records, in turn, make up the file.

A single illustration may help you understand the concepts of a data file, record, and field. Take an address book as an example of a data file. This file would contain name, address, and telephone number data for the individuals appearing in the address book. Each individual's name, address, and phone number would represent one record. For example, the following data would make up one record:

Jay Gatsby
1 Shore Lane
West Egg, NY 10565
516-787-2122

Each individual data item within the record (ie. name, street address, city, state, zip code, telephone number) could be thought of as a field.

A data file is written or read as a series of string or numeric constants. For example, our address book example might be read as follows:

"Jay Gatsby", "1 Shore Lane", "West Egg", "NY", 10565, "516-787-2122"
"Nick Carraway", "7 Shore Lane", "West Egg", "NY", 10565, "516-787-2736"

When these data items are read or written, the first field will have been defined as the name, the second as the street address, the third as the city, the fourth as the state, the fifth as the zip code, and the sixth as the telephone number.

Note that the fifth field is numeric, while the others contain string data. Notice that the string data is enclosed in quotation marks.

Finally, note that each data item is separated by a comma. For the computer to be able to distinguish where one data item ends and another begins, these items must be separated with a character known as a **delimiter.** A delimiter might consist of a comma (as in our example), a blank space, a line return character, or a form feed character.

The advantages of using data files with programs is obvious. Data files allow the user to save, alter, and redisplay data as is necessary. For example, using our address book as an example, programs could be written to do the following:

1. Enter changes in an individual's record by reading the file from storage until the desired record is found, inputting the required changes, and rewriting the file back into storage.

2. Displaying an individual's name, address, and telephone information by reading the file from storage until the desired record is found, outputting the field data to the screen, and rewriting the file back into storage.

The use of a data file with a mass storage device is analogous to the use of a file cabinet for storing information in an office.

File Specifications

Every file is identified with a **file specification,** which consists of a **filename** and a **device name.** Some examples of file specifications are given below:

        CAS1:TEXT
        B:CUSTOMER
        A:LETTER2.TXT

Every file is identified by a filename which can include up to eight characters. These characters can contain the letters A to Z or numbers 0 to 9. Filenames for files being stored on diskette may also include a **filename extension.** A filename extension consists of a period and three letters which appear immediately after the primary filename.

A filename can be entered with upper or lower case letters. However, the computer will interpret all lower case entries as capitals. The following filenames all refer to the same file:

        Vendor.TXT
        VENDOR.txt
        VENDOR.TXT
        vendor.txt

The file specification prefixes the filename with a device name. The device name is the name of the storage device which is to hold the file. We will use the following device names in our discussion:

CAS1: Cassette tape recorder
A: Diskette drive A
B: Diskette drive B

Note that the device name ends with a colon.

When you are using Cassette BASIC the device name need not be included in the file specification. The computer assumes that the device is CAS1: for all filenames.

Opening And Closing A File

A continuation of our analogy between a cassette or diskette file and a file cabinet will help clarify the concept of opening and closing a file. Before a file can be read from a file drawer, that drawer must first be opened. By the same token, when we have finished with a file drawer, we close that drawer.

In much the same manner, program and data files must also be opened and closed. A file is opened with the BASIC statement OPEN. The OPEN statement takes the following format:

OPEN *filespec* [FOR *mode*] AS [1#] *filenumber* [LEN=*rcdlength*]

The abbreviations in the preceding format can be interpreted as follows:

filespec is the file specification.

mode can be any of the following:
INPUT--for sequential input mode (reading the file).
OUTPUT--for sequential output mode (writing the file).

APPEND--for sequential output mode for diskette files only. If the file being OPEN'd does exist, it will be positioned to the end of the existing file. If that file does not exist, it will be created as an output file.

Notice that *mode* is optional (enclosed in brackets [ ]). If mode is not specified, random file access is assumed.

filenumber   is a required number which is used to refer to a file while it is open. It is much easier to refer to a file as #1 than by its file specification.

rcdlength   is used to specify the record length for random files.

The following are examples of valid OPEN statements:

```
OPEN "A:TRANS:DAT" FOR INPUT AS #1
OPEN "B:TEXT.FLE" FOR APPEND AS #2
OPEN "CALENDAR" FOR OUTPUT AS #1
```

The first example opens TRANS.DAT on drive A for input as file #1. The second example opens TEXT.FLE on drive B for an append as file #2. The third example opens CALENDAR on the cassette for output as file #1. Note that the device name was assumed in this example.

The OPEN statement can also be used with the following alternate format:

OPEN *altmode,* [#] *filenumber, filespec* [*,rcdlength*]

The abbreviations in the preceding format can be interpreted as follows:

     altmode   is a string whose first character is one of the following:

        O--indicates sequential output mode.
        I--indicates sequential input mode.
        R--indicates random input/output mode.

    filenumber, filespec, and *rcdlength* retain the same meaning as in the first format.

The following are examples of the use of the alternate format of the OPEN statement:

```
OPEN "O", #1, "B:FILE.DAT"
OPEN "I", #2, "A:VENDOR.DAT"
OPEN "O", #1, "CAS1:CHECKS"
```

The first example opens FILE.DAT as #1 for output on drive B. The second example opens VENDOR.DAT as #2 for input on drive A. The third example opens CHECKS as #1 for output on the cassette device.

IBM BASIC places a limit on the number of files that may be open at any one time. In Cassette BASIC, only one file may be open at a time. In Diskette and Advanced BASIC, the maximum number of open diskette files is specified in the BASIC command entry (as explained at the end of Chapter 1). From 1 to 15 files may be specified as the maximum that can be open at any one time in Diskette or Advanced BASIC. If no entry is made in the BASIC commands, a maximum of three (3) diskette files can be open at any one time.

One rule to keep in mind when working with files is that the same file may not be open for both input and output at the same time. The following statements would cause an error:

```
100 OPEN "A:ACCOUNT.DAT" FOR INPUT AS #1
200 OPEN "A:ACCOUNT.DAT" FOR OUTPUT AS #2
```

To change ACCOUNT.DAT from input to output, the file must first be closed. This could be accomplished by inserting the following statement:

150 CLOSE #1

Once ACCOUNT.DAT has been closed as an input file, it may be reopened as an output file.

It is good programming practice to close a file, once the program has finished accessing it. More than one file can be closed with a single CLOSE statement as illustrated below:

900 CLOSE #2, #3

If the CLOSE statement is executed as shown below,

950 CLOSE

all open files will be closed.

Random And Sequential Access

All cassette files are **sequential** files. Sequential files can only be accessed sequentially. In other words, before the third record can be read, the first and second records must have been read.

The problem with sequential files is obvious. To access any one record in a file, the user must first access all records in the file which precede the record being searched for.

Random access allows more flexible access than sequential files. With random files, the user can read or write any record in a file without first searching through records which precede it.

Random access is available on diskette files, but not on cassette files. Sequential access is available on both diskette and cassette files.

Saving And Loading Programs In Cassette BASIC

As you may remember from Chapter 2, only one BASIC program can be held in RAM at any one time. When the NEW command is entered, the program currently held in RAM is erased so that a new program can be entered.

If you wish to save a program held in RAM for future use, you can do so with the SAVE command. The following SAVE command will save CALCULATE on the cassette tape unit:

SAVE "CALCULATE"

Notice that we did not use the device name for the cassette unit (CAS1:) in the file specification. If the device name is omitted in Cassette BASIC, CAS1: is assumed. CAS1: is the only device name allowed in Cassette BASIC.

The LOAD command can be later used to load a program from the cassette tape unit into RAM so that it can be run. LOAD takes the following format:

LOAD *file specification* [,R]

file specification   is the file specification of the file to be loaded. Again, in Cassette BASIC, CAS1: is assumed to be the device. R is an optional parameter that causes the program to be automatically executed after it is loaded.

When LOAD is executed in the direct mode, the filenames on the cassette tape will be displayed on the screen one by one. If the current file does not match the file named in *file specification*, the message "Skipped" will be displayed. If the file specified is found, the message "Found" will be displayed. If the LOAD command is executed within a BASIC program, the filenames found and skipped will not be displayed on the screen.

The loading process may be ended at any time by pressing the Control and Break keys simultaneously. BASIC will exit to the direct mode with the previous contents of RAM remaining unchanged.

The following LOAD command will load the cassette file "CHECKBOOK", but will not execute it:

LOAD "CHECKBOOK"

By including the optional parameter, R, CHECKBOOK will be both loaded and automatically executed.

LOAD "CHECKBOOK", R

The following version of the LOAD command will load the next program on the tape:

LOAD "CAS1:"

Using Data Files On Cassette Units

In this section, we will discuss the programming procedures for sending a data file to a cassette tape device or inputting data from a cassette tape device.

Once a file has been opened with the OPEN statement, the WRITE# statement is used to send a data file to the cassette tape unit. The WRITE# statement takes the following format:

WRITE# *filenumber, expressions*

filenumber refers to the number assigned to the file when it was opened. *expressions* can be either string or numeric constants or variables. These will be output to the specified file.

The following are examples of valid WRITE# statements:

WRITE #1, "John", "Bill", "Dave", "Willie", "Bruce"
WRITE #1, X1, X2, X3, Z$

The first WRITE statement will write the 5 string constants specified to the cassette file. The second WRITE statement will write the values of the variables specified to the cassette file.

When writing data to a cassette file, the WRITE# statement automatically delimits strings with quotation marks, inserts commas as delimiters between data items, and enters a carriage return character after the final data item. Delimiters need not be inserted between the expressions themselves in the WRITE# statement.

Data files are read from the cassette tape device with the INPUT# statement. Data items may only be read from a cassette file in the order in which that data was written. Therefore, to read a cassette file, the user will be required to know the format used to write the file. Also, to read one particular data item, other items which precede it in the file may have to be read first.

The program in Illustration 5-1 illustrates the use of the INPUT# statement. In this example, we are assuming that ADDRESS is a cassette file with 5 alphanumeric and 1 numeric field.

Note the use of the EOF function in the example in Illustration 5-1. EOF is used to check for the end-of-file condition. In our example, if the end of the file had been reached without a match being found, the program would have attempted to read a file that contained no more data. This would have resulted in an error condition.

Using IBM BASIC With Diskette Files

In this section, we will discuss the usage of IBM BASIC with diskette files. The versions of IBM BASIC that can be used with diskette files are Disk BASIC and Advanced BASIC.

Before covering the disk file handling commands used in Disk BASIC and Advanced BASIC, we will discuss the usage of floppy diskettes in general as well as some of the concepts of DOS-- IBM's disk operating system.

Illustration 5-1. Use Of INPUT# With Cassette Files

```
Ok
100  OPEN "CAS1:ADDRESS" FOR INPUT AS #1
200  INPUT "ENTER PHONE NUMBER DESIRED"; Z$
250  IF EOF (1) THEN 1200
300  INPUT #1, A$, B$, C$, D$, E, F$
400  IF F$ = Z$ THEN 500 ELSE 250
500  CLS
600  PRINT A$
700  PRINT B$
800  PRINT C$; ","; D$; " "; E
900  PRINT F$
1000 PRINT
1100 PRINT "THIS IS THE PERSON YOU ARE
         LOOKING FOR"
1200 END
RUN
  ENTER PHONE NUMBER DESIRED? 516-787-2122

  JAY GATSBY
  1 SHORE LANE
  WEST EGG, NY 10565
  516-787-2122

  THIS IS THE PERSON YOU ARE LOOKING FOR
```

Floppy Diskette Usage

Either one or two diskette drives may be installed on your IBM PC. In this and the following section, we will explain a few of the fundamentals of diskette and DOS usage. These concepts are explained in detail in another WSI text, User's Guide To The IBM Personal Computer.

Your IBM PC disk drives will be identified with the letters A and B. The drive on the right side is drive A. The one on the left is drive B. The IBM PC diskette drives are designed to use 5¼″ floppy diskettes (also known as mini-floppy diskettes). Each diskette can hold about 163,000 characters (or 160K). This is the equivalent of approximately 50 double spaced pages of typewritten text.

A diagram of a 5¼ inch floppy diskette is depicted in Illustration 5-2. the diskette itself is sealed within a protective jacket. The diskette can rotate within this jacket. Do not attempt to open this protective jacket.

Information is read from or written to the diskette via the read/write opening in the jacket. Do not touch the surface of the diskette which is exposed beneath the read/write opening. Also, be careful not to allow this exposed portion of the diskette to become scratched.

The write protect notch allows the user to prevent information from being written onto the diskette. If the write protect notch is covered with a foil adhesive tab (provided with diskettes), that diskette can be read from, but it can not be written onto. To write on a mini-floppy diskette, the write protect notch must be uncovered.

When inserting a diskette into the diskette drive, first of all, open the diskette drive door. The label side of the diskette should be facing up and the write protect notch should be to your left. Once the diskette has been inserted, close the drive door.

Remember that diskettes are fragile and easily damaged. Observe the following rules when handling diskettes.

1. Never touch the exposed surface of a diskette.

2. Never clean or dust the exposed surface of a diskette.

3. Do not allow the exposed surface of a diskette to become scratched.

4. Store diskettes in a vertical position.

Illustration 5-2. 5¼ Inch Floppy Diskette

5. Protect diskettes from sources of heat or light.

6. Do not bend a diskette.

7. Never write on a diskette with a pencil, pen, or any other sharp pointed writing instrument. Use a felt tipped pen to write on a diskette.

8. Keep diskette clear from magnetic fields such as telephones, radios, televisions, and tape recorders. A magnetic field might cause data on the diskette to be erased.

9. Never remove a diskette from the drive while the drive is still running. When the drive is running, the drive's in use light will be on, and its motor will be running.

Storing DOS

The Disk Operating System, or DOS, controls the flow of information between the computer, the keyboard, any peripherals, and the diskette drives. DOS is contained on the DOS diskette which is supplied with your IBM PC when diskette drives are installed in the computer.

Do not use the master copy of your DOS diskette for every day use. Make back-up copies of your DOS master diskette and use these back-up copies for everyday use. The original DOS master should be stored in a safe place for making any additional back-up copies that may be needed. The procedures for making back-up copies of the DOS diskette will be outlined in the next section.

To start DOS, follow these procedures:

1. Insert the DOS diskette in drive A and close the drive door.

2. Turn on any peripherals (ie. monitor, printer, or other devices).

3. Turn on system unit.

4. Diskette A will begin running, after which the date will

be prompted for. Enter the date as per the following example:

06/31/82

Note that dashes may be used in place of the slashes, and that the year may be entered as 1982 instead of 82.

5. The DOS prompt (A>) will now be displayed. This indicates that DOS is ready to accept the entry of commands. The letter A signifies that the current drive is drive A. In other words, if a command is entered without a drive identifier, the computer will assume that that command is to be undertaken on drive A.

6. Enter the BASIC command as described in Chapter 1, and the BASIC prompt (Ok) will be displayed.

Copying Your DOS Master Diskette

As we mentioned previously, you should use a copy of your DOS diskette for everyday use and store your master copy in a safe place. In fact, it is a good practice to make copies of all of your important diskettes. This will prevent accidental loss of your program and data files. The following steps should be followed in copying diskettes in a single diskette system.

1. Enter the following:

A>FORMAT A:

2. DOS will display the following message:

Insert new diskette for drive A:
and strike any key when ready

Remove the diskette that is to be copied and replace it with a blank diskette. Press any key.

3. The blank diskette will then be formatted. When the following message is displayed,

> Formatting...Format Complete
> Format another (Y/N)?

the formatting process will have been completed. The blank diskette is now ready to be copied. Press N and proceed to Step 4.

4. Next, remove the blank diskette and replace it with the diskette from which a copy is to be made. If this diskette does not have a copy of DOS on it, insert a diskette with a copy of DOS. Then, enter the following:

A>DISKCOPY ◢

After this entry has been made, the following message will be displayed:

> Insert source diskette in drive A
> Strike any key when ready

DISKCOPY is a DOS program which can be used to copy any diskette to another diskette.

When the preceding message appears, be certain that the diskette which you want copied is in the diskette drive. Press any key.

5. A portion of the diskette in the drive will then be copied into RAM. When as much data as possible has been copied, the following message will be displayed:

```
Insert target diskette in drive A
Strike any key when ready
```

Remove the diskette from which the copy is being made and insert the blank formatted diskette in the diskette drive. When any key is pressed, the data in RAM will be copied to the blank diskette.

If there is additional data on the source diskette to be copied, steps 4 and 5 will be repeated until all the data has been copied. After all the data has been copied, the following message will be displayed:

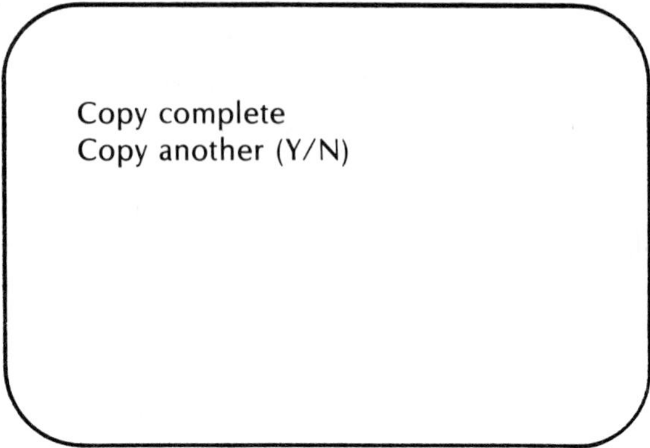

If N is entered, the DOS prompt (A>) will be displayed. The diskette copied to will be an exact duplicate of the original diskette.

In the preceding five steps, we have outlined the procedures necessary for formatting and copying a diskette with a system with one diskette drive. If your system has two drives, you should insert the blank diskette in drive B and the diskette to be copied from in drive A. Enter the following variation of the DISKCOPY command in Step 4,

A><u>DISKCOPY A: B:</u> ↵

and proceed with the remaining steps. The diskette copying process is much easier when a system has two drives rather than one.

Verifying DISKCOPY

It is a good programming practice to check the accuracy of a DISKCOPY operation when important files are being copied. The DOS DISKCOMP commands allow two diskettes to be compared.

If you are using DISKCOMP with a single drive system, you will be prompted (as in DISKCOPY) when to insert the proper diskettes in the drive. If you are using DISKCOMP with a two drive system, insert the two diskettes in drives A and B and enter the following:

A>_DISKCOMP A: B:_

DISKCOMP compares the contents of the two diskettes for all 40 tracks. If DISKCOMP discovers a discrepency between the two diskettes, it will display a message giving the track number (0-39) where the discrepency was found.

When the DISKCOMP operation has been completed, the following prompt will be displayed:

Compare more diskettes? (Y/N)

Press N to end DISKCOMP. If Y is pressed, the user will be prompted to enter the proper diskettes, after which another DISKCOMP will be performed.

System Level

As mentioned previously, DOS manages the flow of data between the diskette drives, the computer, and its peripherals. The user communicates with DOS in what is known as the **system level.** The computer is in the system level whenever the DOS prompt (A> or B>) is displayed.

While at the system level, the user can enter any of the DOS commands such as DISKCOPY and DISKCOMP. The user can not enter BASIC commands while he is at the system level. He must first enter the BASIC command to activate BASIC as described in Chapter 1.

DOS commands can not be used while BASIC is active. If you are in BASIC and you wish to return to the system level, you can do so by entering the following,

SYSTEM

and then pressing Enter. If BASIC is exited to go to DOS, any program currently held in RAM will be erased, unless a SAVE statement (described later) has been executed before exiting BASIC.

More DOS Commands

In this section, we will briefly describe several essential DOS commands. For a complete discussion of IBM DOS, refer to the User's Guide To The IBM Personal Computer published by Weber Systems Inc.

One DOS command that is used frequently is the DIR (for Directory) command. DIR lists the names of all of the files contained on a specified diskette. The following version of the DIR command,

A>DIR

would be used to list the files on drive A.

The ERASE command is used to erase files from the diskette. The following command entry would erase TEXT.DAT from drive A:

A>ERASE TEXT.DAT

The RENAME command is used to rename a file. The following command would be used to rename TEXT as NEWTEXT:

A>RENAME TEXT NEWTEXT

Remember, the old name always precedes the new name in the RENAME command.

The TYPE command can be used to send the contents of a file to the screen. The following command would send VENDOR.DAT to the screen from drive B:

A>TYPE B:VENDOR.DAT

By pressing the Control and PRTSC key simultaneously before

the TYPE command is entered, the file will be sent to the printer as well as to the screen.

The COPY command is used to copy one or more diskette files. The following COPY command entry would copy EXAMPLE.TXT from drive B to drive A.

A><u>COPY B:EXAMPLE.TXT</u> 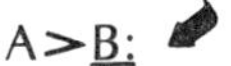

The following variation of the COPY command would copy ACCOUNT.DAT from drive A to drive B.

A><u>COPY ACCOUNT.DAT B:</u>

The COPY command has many more variations which are beyond the scope of our discussion. For our purposes, COPY should be thought of as a DOS command which allows individual diskette files to be copied.

Changing The Current Drive

As mentioned earlier, the DOS prompt indicates which drive is the **current** or **default** drive. If a DOS or BASIC command is entered without specifying which diskette drive it is to apply to, DOS or BASIC will assume that the command applies to the current drive.

For example, if the current drive was A, and the following BASIC command was executed,

SAVE "TEXT.DAT"

TEXT.DAT will be saved on drive A.

The following command will change the current drive from A to B:

A><u>B:</u>

If you wish to change the current drive from B to A, you can do so with the following entry:

B>A: ◄

Saving And Loading Diskette Files

The SAVE command is used to save a program from RAM onto diskette. The drive identifier must be included in the file specification used with SAVE. For example, the following command would be used to save the program file ACCOUNT.BAS on drive A:

SAVE "A:ACCOUNT.BAS"

The LOAD command is used to load a diskette program from diskette back into RAM. If a drive identifier is not included in the file specification, the current disk drive will be assumed. If no filename extension is included in the file specification, an extension of .BAS will be assumed. If the optional parameter R is included in the LOAD command, the program will be automatically run after it has been loaded.

The following LOAD command will load and execute ACCOUNT.BAS from drive A:

LOAD "A:ACCOUNT",R

Notice that the filename extension .BAS was not supplied, but was assumed.

Using Data Files With Diskette Systems

A diskette data file, like a cassette data file, must have been opened via the OPEN statement before data can be read from or written to it.

Once a file has been opened with the OPEN statement, information can be read from or written to that file with the INPUT# and WRITE# statements. These are used in much the same manner as with cassette data files.

One point to keep in mind when writing to a data file is that if you wish to add data to the end of an existing file, that file must have been opened for APPEND not for OUTPUT. If the user attempts to write new data to an existing file opened for OUTPUT, the new data entries will destroy the previous data. If the file was opened for APPEND, the new data will be added to the end of the existing file.

CHAPTER 6.
ADVANCED CONCEPTS

Introduction

In this chapter, we will discuss some advanced IBM BASIC programming concepts. These include the use of the Alt key, program entry and editing, and program error debugging.

Alt Key And BASIC

The Alt key has a special use in BASIC, in that it allows the user to enter entire BASIC keywords with only one keystroke. The BASIC keywords listed in Table 6-1 will be typed when the associated alphabetic key is pressed while the Alt key is being held down.

The Alt key can also be used to enter valid ASCII characters not found on the keyboard. This is accomplished by holding the Alt key while entering the three digit ASCII code for the desired character on the numeric key pad.

Entering a BASIC Program

BASIC programs are entered as **program lines.** Any text preceded with a number (**line number**) and ended by pressing the Enter key will be regarded as a program line.

The maximum number of characters that may be included in any one line is 255 including Enter. If a line contains more than 255 characters, those extra characters will be dropped, or **truncated,** when Enter is pressed.

BASIC key words and variable names can be entered in lower case, upper case, or a combination of both. However, these entries will be converted to upper case by the BASIC program editor.

Table 6-1. Alt/Alpha BASIC Keyword Abbreviations

A	AUTO	N	NEXT
B	BSAVE	O	OPEN
C	COLOR	P	PRINT
D	DELETE	Q	(no word)
E	ELSE	R	RUN
F	FOR	S	SCREEN
G	GOTO	T	THEN
H	HEX$	U	USING
I	INPUT	V	VAL
J	(no word)	W	WIDTH
K	KEY	X	XOR
L	LOCATE	Y	(no word)
M	MOTOR	Z	(no word)

A new line can be added to a BASIC program by merely entering a line number followed by the desired text and Enter. When Enter is pressed, the line will be saved as part of the BASIC program.

A line can be replaced in a BASIC program by entering the same line number followed by the desired text and Enter. The new entry will replace the previous line.

To delete a line in an existing program, merely enter the line number of the line to be deleted followed by Enter. A group of lines can be deleted via the DELETE command, and an entire program can be deleted with the NEW command. These will be discussed in the next chapter.

The methods just described for entering a BASIC program only change the program in memory. To save the program with the changes, the SAVE command must be used.

Editing An IBM BASIC Program

Once you have entered a program, you may discover an error and need to change or edit it. One way to make corrections is to retype the entire line that contains the error.

Fortunately, however, there is a much easier way to edit program lines. The IBM PC's **line editor** or **editor** allows the user to insert, delete, or change text within a program line.

The editing of a program line consists of the following three steps:

1. Locate the position where the change is to be made.

2. Enter the change via the keyboard.

3. Send the change to RAM by pressing the Enter key.

These three steps are accomplished with a group of special editing keys. The majority of these keys are located on the numeric keypad. When the NUMLOCK key is depressed, the numeric keypad can be used for entering numbers. When the NUMLOCK key is not depressed, the numeric keypad keys can be used for editing purposes.

Each editing key has a symbol or group of letters on it, such as ←, →, ↑, ↓, DEL, etc. These symbolize that key's editing function. The BASIC program editing keys are summarized in Table 6-2.

Table 6-2. BASIC Program Editor Keys

Key	Function
Home	This key can be used to move the cursor to the upper lefthand position on the screen.
Ctrl-Home	This key combination clears the screen and positions the cursor to the "home" position.
↑	Moves cursor up one row (Cursor-Up).
↓	Moves cursor down by one row (Cursor-Down).
←	Moves cursor one position to the left. If the cursor is positioned to the leftmost position, it will 'wrap around' to the rightmost position of the preceding line (Cursor Left).

Table 6-2. BASIC Program Editor Keys (Cont.)

Key	Description
⟶	Moves cursor one position to the right. If the cursor is in the rightmost position, it will move to the leftmost position of the next line down (Cursor Right).
Ctrl⟶	Moves cursor to the next word. Words are groups of characters which begin with either a letter or a number and are separated from other words by blanks or special characters. Ctrl⟶ is also known as next word.
Ctrl⟵	This key combination is also known as previous word. It moves the cursor to the previous word.
End	Moves the cursor to the end of the logical line.
Ctrl-End	Erases from the cursor position to the end of the logical line.
Ins	This sets the insert mode. If the insert mode was off, pressing Ins turns it on. If the insert mode was on, pressing this key turns it on. If the flashing cursor covers the lower half character position, the insert mode is on. The insert mode is also turned off when the user presses any of the cursor movement keys or Enter.
Del	This key deletes the characters at the current cursor position. All characters to the right of the deleted character are moved one position to the left to fill the space left empty by the deleted character.

Table 6-2. BASIC Program Editor Keys (Cont.)

Backspace ←	The Backspace key is identified by ←(like the Cursor Left key). However, the Backspace key is located directly to the left of the NUMLOCK key. The Backspace key results in the deletion of the last character typed. In other words, the character to the left of the cursor will be erased. The characters to the right of the one deleted will be moved one position to the right to fill the empty position.
ESC	This key will cause the entire line to be erased from the screen when it is pressed anywhere within that line. If the line is a program line, it will not be erased from the program in memory.
Ctrl-Break	This key combination causes the program to return to the direct mode. Any changes made to the line being edited will not be saved.
→|	The Tab key moves the cursor to the next tab stop. Tab stops occur every eight character positions. When the insert mode is on, pressing the Tab key causes blanks to be inserted from the current cursor position to the next tab stop.

Editing Example

The best way to illustrate the editing process is with the use of an example. Suppose that the following program lines had been typed in:

```
100  DASA 200, 300, 400, 500, 600
200  READ A, B, C, D, E
__
```

The underline in line 3 indicates the position of the cursor.

Our example contains an obvious error; the misspelling of DATA. Also, we wish to insert 100, before 200 in line 100, and also delete ,600 from the end of the same line.

Our first step is to position the cursor at the position of the first error. The following keys can be used to move the cursor:

↑ Cursor up one line
↓ Cursor down one line
← Cursor left one character
→ Cursor right one character

Additional cursor control keys are described in Table 6-2, but in our example, we will concentrate on these four.

To correct the error in line 100, we would first press the ↑ key twice and then press the → key 6 times. The cursor would now be positioned as follows:

```
100  DASA 200, 300, 400, 500, 600
200  READ A, B, C, D, E
```

Step 1 of the editing process has now been accomplished. The cursor is positioned over the error. We are now ready to execute Step 2 by typing in the change. In this case, we merely type in T. The T will replace the S. The following will then be displayed:

```
100  DATA 200, 300, 400, 500, 600
200  READ A, B, C, D, E
```

We could press Enter at this point to send the change into RAM. However, since we have 2 additional corrections (The insertion of 100, and the deletion of ,600), we will continue editing.

First of all, we will move the cursor two spaces to the right by pressing the →key twice. The display will then appear as follows:

        100 DATA 200, 300, 400, 500, 600
        200 READ A, B, C, D, E

At this point, we wish to insert 100, in the DATA list. To do this, we press the Ins (Insert) key and enter the data to be inserted (100,). The new text will be entered at the current cursor position, and all existing text will move to the right. The display will now appear as follows:

        100 DATA 100, 200, 300, 400, 500, 600
        200 READ A, B, C, D, E

Once the required data has been inserted, the insert mode should be cancelled. This is done by pressing the Ins key once again. We can now make more corrections on the same line.

Another way to cancel the insert mode is to press the Enter key. However, doing so sends the current program line to RAM. Since we have one final correction on the current line, we will turn off the insert mode by pressing the Ins key a second time.

Our final correction is to delete ,600 from line 100. First, the cursor should be positioned under the comma preceding 600 by pressing the → key the required number of times.

We are now ready to delete ,600. This is accomplished by pressing the Del key 4 times. Every time the Del key is pressed, the character at the cursor position is deleted and the remainder of the text in the line is moved one position to the left. After pressing the Del key 4 times, our display is as follows:

        100 DATA 100, 200, 300, 400, 500__
        200 READ A, B, C, D, E

Since the needed corrections have been made, we are now ready to send line 100 to memory. This is accomplished by pressing the Enter key.

Errors & Debugging In IBM BASIC

An error in a program is also known as a bug. The process of finding and correcting these bugs is known as debugging. Debugging can be a very laborious process. Fortunately, IBM BASIC is equipped with a number of features which help make debugging easier.

Most bugs cause program execution to stop. In these cases, an error message will be displayed which indicates the type of error encountered as well as the line number where the error occurred. The following is an example of an error message. This message is displayed as a result of a NEXT statement being encountered without a corresponding FOR statement:

NEXT without FOR in 750

Appendix C contains a list of the IBM BASIC error messages.

You may also encounter situations where your program executes without an error message, but you know that an error exists because the program is not operating as you desired. These errors are known as **logic** errors and are more difficult to diagnose than errors in which an error message is displayed.

One tool that can prove very useful in tracking down logic errors is the trace flag. The trace flag causes the line number as well as the output to be printed as each line is executed. The line numbers are enclosed in brackets. This allows the user to trace the execution of the program line by line, and, hopefully, discover where any logic error occurs.

The trace flag is enabled by entering the TRON (Trace On) command. The trace flag is disabled by entering the TROFF (Trace Off) command. Illustration 6-1 contains a sample run of a program using the trace flag.

Illustration 6-1. TRON, TROFF Example

```
Ok
100  X = 100
200  FOR I = 1 TO 3
300  X = 2 * X
400  PRINT X
500  NEXT
600  END
TRON
Ok
RUN
[100] [200] [300] [400] 200
[500] [300] [400] 400
[500] [300] [400] 800
[500] [600]
Ok
TROFF
Ok
```

CHAPTER 7.
REFERENCE GUIDE

Introduction

In this chapter, we will provide descriptions of the various commands, statements, and functions used in IBM BASIC.

The following rules and abbreviations will be followed in this chapter in our configuaration descriptions of the various BASIC commands, statements, and functions.

1. Any capitalized words are keywords. These may be input in either uppercase, lowercase, or both. BASIC automatically converts keywords to uppercase.

2. Any words, phrases, or letters shown in lowercase italics identify an entry that must be made by the operator.

3. Any items enclosed in brackets [ ] are optional.

4. An ellipsis (...) shows that an item may be repeated as often as desired.

5. Any punctuation marks, except the square brackets, (ex. ; , =) must be included where they are shown.

6. The following abbreviations may be used in this chapter:

numexp	any numeric expression
intexp	any integer expression
$$$exp	any string expression

ABS

- Cassette
- Disk
- Advanced

The ABS function will return the absolute value of its argument.

Configuration

$a = ABS(b)$

Example

```
Ok
PRINT ABS(-11)
 11
Ok
```

ASC

- Cassette
- Disk
- Advanced

The ASC function returns the ASCII code for the first character of its string argument.

Configuration

$a = ASC(\$\$\$exp)$

If the string argument of the ASC function is a null string, an "Illegal function call" error will be returned.

Example

```
Ok
100 X$ = "ABC"
200 PRINT ASC(X$)
RUN
 65
Ok
```

ATN

- Cassette
- Disk
- Advanced

The ATN function returns the arctangent of its argument.

Configuration

a = ATN(b)

Example

```
Ok
100 X = 5
200 PRINT ATN(X)
RUN
 1.373400
Ok
```

AUTO

- Cassette
- Disk
- Advanced

The AUTO command results in a new line number being generated every time the user presses the Enter key.

Configuration

AUTO [*number*] [,] [*increment*]

where;

number is the beginning line number

increment is the amount to be added to the previous line number to generate the next, new line number.

The AUTO command is generally used when entering programs. This saves the user the task of typing every line number.

If no parameters are included in the AUTO command, the beginning line number will be 10 and each new line number generated will be incremented by 10.

If a beginning line number is specified in the AUTO command followed by a comma, but the increment is not specified, the last increment specified in an AUTO command will be used. If an increment is specified with a comma preceding it, but no beginning line number is specified, the beginning line number will be 0.

If a period (.) is substituted for the beginning line number, the current line will be used as the beginning line number.

The AUTO command might generate a line number that already exists in the program. If this occurs, an asterisk (*) will be printed immediately following the line number. This is meant as a warning to the user. If any data is input into that line, the existing program line will be replaced by it. If the user presses the Enter key immediately after the asterisk without entering any new data, a new line number will be generated, and the existing line will not be replaced.

The AUTO command is ended by pressing the Ctrl-Break key combination. The current line being entered when Ctrl-Break is pressed will be erased. After Ctrl-Break has been pressed, BASIC will return to the command level.

Example

```
AUTO
AUTO 100,20
AUTO 1000
AUTO, 100
```

The first command will generate the line numbers 0, 10, 20, 30, ... The second command will generate the line numbers 100, 120, 140,....The third command will generate the line numbers, 1000, 1020, 1040, 1060,....Since the increment for the preceding AUTO command was 20, the same increment will be used for the third AUTO command. The line numbers generated by the final AUTO command will be 0, 100, 200, and so on.

BEEP

■ Cassette
■ Disk
■ Advanced

The BEEP statement is used to cause the speaker to beep.

Configuration

BEEP

Example

100 IF X = Y THEN BEEP

BLOAD

■ Cassette
■ Disk
■ Advanced

BLOAD can be used to load any segment defined as the source file by the DEF SEG statement. The BLOAD command is generally used for loading machine language programs.

Configuration

BLOAD *filespec* [*,offset*]

Where;

filespec refers to the file specification for the file being loaded.

offset refers to the address at which loading is to start. This address is designated as an offset into the segment specified in the last DEF SEG statement.

BLOAD With Cassette BASIC

Unless a device name is specified, the device CAS1: will be assumed. When BLOAD is executed in the direct mode, the filenames for the files on the cassette tape will be listed one by one on the screen. These filenames will be followed by a period and one of the following letters (which indicate the file type).

.B indicates a BASIC program stored in internal format and created by the SAVE command.

.P indicates a protected BASIC program in internal format and created with the SAVE .P command.

.A indicates a BASIC program in ASCII format and created via the SAVE .A command.

.M indicates a memory image file created with the BSAVE command.

.D indicates a data file created by the OPEN statement.

As the files are displayed on the screen, they will be followed by one of the following messages:

Skipped
Found

"Skipped" indicates the file displayed does not match the file named in BLOAD.
"Found" indicates that the file displayed was named in BLOAD.

If BLOAD is executed in a BASIC program, the filenames will not be displayed on the screen.

BLOAD With Disk Or Advanced BASIC

If the device name is not included, the current disk drive is assumed to be the device.

BSAVE

The BSAVE command makes it possible to save a part of memory on a device. Generally, BSAVE is used for saving machine language programs.

Configuration

BSAVE *filespec, offset, length*

Where;

    filespec is the file specification for the file to be saved.

    offset is the offset in the segment last designated by the previous DEF SEG statement. This is where saving will begin.

    length is the length of the memory image to be saved.

If you are using Cassette BASIC, the device CAS1: will be assumed, and a memory image file will be written on the magnetic tape.

If you are using Disk or Advanced BASIC, the designated device name will receive the file. If no device name is given, the current drive will receive the file.

CALL

The Call statement is used to call a machine language subroutine.

Configuration

CALL *numericvar* [(*variable* [,*variable*]...)]

Where;

numericvar designates the name of a numeric variable, the value of which gives the starting address in memory of the subroutine being CALL'ed. This address is given as an offset into the current segment of memory (i.e. the one given in the last DEF SEG statement).

variable refers to the name of a variable which is to be given as an argument to the machine language subroutine.

Example

```
1000  DEF SEG = &H6000
1100  A = 0
1200  CALL A(X, Y$, Z)
```

In the preceding example, the segment is set to location hex 6000 in line 1000. A is set to zero which results in the call to A executing the subroutine at location hex 6000.

CDBL

■ Cassette
■ Disk
■ Advanced

The CDBL function is used to convert its argument to a double-precision number.

Configuration

a = CDBL(*b*)

Example

```
Ok
100  A = 367.55
200  PRINT A; CDBL(A)
RUN
    367.55      367.5498767101423
Ok
```

CHAIN

□ Cassette
■ Disk
■ Advanced

The CHAIN statement is used to transfer program control to another program.

Configuration

CHAIN [MERGE] *filespec* [,[*line*] [,[ALL] [,DELETE *range*]]]

Where;

filespec refers to the name of the program that is to be CHAIN'ed.

line refers to a line number within the program being CHAIN'ed. That is the point within that program where excution is to begin.

If the MERGE option is included, a section of the code may be brought into the BASIC program as an overlay. In other words, a MERGE operation will be performed with the current program and the program being CHAIN'ed. The program being CHAIN'ed must be an ASCII file if it is to be MERGE'd (see explanation of MERGE command on page 225).

An example of the use of the MERGE command in a CHAIN statement is given below;

CHAIN MERGE "A:NEW", 1000

In this example, the program NEW on drive A will be brought

into the program as an overlay with a starting point for execution in line 1000.

Once an overlay has been used, it is generally deleted so that a new overlay can be instituted. This is accomplished with the DELETE option. The DELETE option, when used in the CHAIN statement, functions much like the DELETE command.

In the following example,

CHAIN MERGE "A:NEW", 1000, DELETE 1000-3000

lines 1000 through 3000 in the current program will be deleted before the loading of the overlay.

The ALL option passes every variable in the current program to the program being CHAIN'ed. In cases where the ALL option is not included in the CHAIN statement, the current program must contain a COMMON statement which lists all variables that are to be passed to the programs being CHAIN'ed.

CHR$

■ Cassette
■ Disk
■ Advanced

The CHR$ function is used to convert an ASCII code to its corresponding character.

Configuration

$a\$ = CHR\$(b)$

where b is a number or numeric expression from 0 to 255.

CHR$ is often used to send a special character to either the screen or the printer.

Example

```
Ok
100  LPRINTER
200  PRINT CHR$(33)
      .
      .
RUN
```

In the preceding example, the exclamation point is sent to the line printer.

CINT

■ Cassette
■ Disk
■ Advanced

The CINT function is used to convert its argument to an integer.

Configuration

$$a = CINT(b)$$

The fractional portion of the argument will be rounded to determine the integer result.

Example

```
Ok
PRINT CINT(15.46)
  15
Ok
```

CIRCLE

□ Cassette
□ Disk
■ Advanced

The CIRCLE statement is used in the graphics mode to draw an ellipse on the screen.

Configuration

CIRCLE (*xcenter, ycenter*), *radius* [,*color* [,*start* , *end* [,*aspect*]]]

Where;

x center
y center gives the center of the ellipse.

radius gives the radius of the ellipse.

color refers to the foreground color. The default value for color is 3 in medium resolution and 1 in high resolution.

start,end refers to the points where the drawing of the ellipse will begin and end. These are given in radians and may range from –2*PI to 2*PI where PI = 3.141593. If the start or end angle is negative, the ellipse will be connected to its center point with a line. The angles will be regarded as being positive.

aspect affects the ratio of the x-radius to the y-radius. The default value for aspect is 5/6 in medium resolution and 5/12 in high resolution.

If the aspect given is less than 1, the radius given is the x-radius. In other words, the radius is measured in points in the horizontal direction. If the aspect given is greater than one, the y-radius will be given.

CLEAR

■ Cassette
■ Disk
■ Advanced

The Clear command is used to set all numeric variables to zero and to set all string variables to null. Clear can also optionally be used to set the end of memory and the amount of stack space.

Configuration

CLEAR [,[exp1] [,exp2]]

Where;

exp1 is a byte count which sets the maximum number of bytes available for BASIC to store programs and data files.

exp2 reserves stack space for BASIC. The default value is

either 512 bytes or one eighth of available memory--
whichever is smaller.

CLOSE

■ Cassette
■ Disk
■ Advanced

the Close statement is used to end input and/or output to the
specified device or file.

Configuration

CLOSE [[#] *filenum* [,[#] *filenum*]...]

Where;

> filenum refers to the number of the file which was used in the
> **Open statement.**

If the Close statement is used without an optional file number, all
devices and files which were open will be closed.

CLS

■ Cassette
■ Disk
■ Advanced

The CLS statement is used to clear the screen.

Configuration

CLS

The CLS statement also causes the cursor to return to the home
position. In the text mode, this is the upper left hand corner of
the screen. In the graphics mode, this is the point in the center of
the screen (160,100--medium resolution; 320,100--high
resolution).

Also, if the screen is in the text mode, the active page will be cleared to the background color. If the screen is in the graphics mode, the screen buffer will be cleared to the background color.

COLOR

■ Cassette
■ Disk
■ Advanced

The Color statement is used to set the colors for the foreground, background, and border screen. The usage of the Color statement differs depending on whether the text mode or graphics mode is being used. This is set by the Screen statement.

The text mode allows the user to set the following:

Foreground	1 of 16 colors
Background	1 of 8 colors
Border	1 of 16 colors

The border is an area on the TV set or monitor which is outside the area used for characters. The color for the border can be set with the Color statement.

Every character on the screen consists of two portions; the foreground and the background. The foreground is the actual character, while the background is a box that outlines the character.

In the graphics mode, the user can set the following:

Background	1 of 16 colors
Palette	1 of 2 palettes of 3 colors each

In the graphics mode, the border is the same color as the background.

Configuration (Text Mode)

COLOR [*foreground*] [,[*background*] [,*border*]]

Where;

foreground is the color of the character and must be a number or numeric expression from 0 to 31.

background is the color of the background and must be a number or numeric expression from 0 to 7.

border is the color for the border screen and must be a number from 0 to 15.

The following colors are available for *foreground* if the color/graphics monitor adapter is being used.

0	Black	8	Gray
1	Blue	9	Light Blue
2	Green	10	Light Green
3	Cyan	11	Light Cyan
4	Red	12	Light Red
5	Magenta	13	Light Magenta
6	Brown	14	Yellow
7	White	15	High Intensity White

By selecting the *foreground* equal to 16 plus the color desired, the character will blink. In other words, a value of 22 will result in brown blinking.

Colors 0 through 7 can be selected for *background*.

If you are using the IBM Monochrome Display and Printer Adapter, the following can be used for *foreground*.

0	Black
1	Underline character with white foreground
7	White
15	High Intensity White

Again, by adding 16 to the desired value, the character will blink. For example, 16 will result in black blinking.

With the IBM Monochrome Display and Printer Adapter, either

of the following may be used for *background*.

0   Black
7   White

Example

100 COLOR 2,7,0

In the preceding example, the *foreground* is set to green, the *background* is set to white, and the *border* is set to black.

Configuration (Graphics Mode)

COLOR [*background*] [,[*palette*]]

Where;

background is the background and must be a number or numeric expression from 0 to 15.

palette is the selection of a palette of available colors and must be either 0 or 1 or an expression evaluating to those values.

The COLOR statement will set the colors used by the PSET, PRESET, LINE, CIRCLE, PAINT, and DRAW statements.

The *background* colors allowed are 0 through 15 in the list given previously. The palette selections available are given in Table 7-1.

If palette 0 is chosen, color number 1 will be green, color 2 will be red, and color 3 will be brown. If palette 1 is chosen, color 1 will be cyan, color 2 will be magenta, and color 3 will be white.

Table 7-1. Palette Color Selections

Color #	Palette 0	Palette 1
1	Green	Cyan
2	Red	Magenta
3	Brown	White

The Color statement can only be used in medium resolution. Attempting to use the Color statement in the high resolution mode will result in an "Illegal function call" error.

Example

100 SCREEN 1
200 COLOR 8,0

In the preceding example, the background is set to grey and palette 0 is selected.

□ Cassette
□ Disk
■ Advanced

COM

The COM statement is used to allow or disallow the trapping of communications on the Communications Adapter.

Configuration

COM(*n*) ON
COM(*n*) OFF
COM(*n*) STOP

Where;

  n is the number of the communications adapter (1 or 2)

Before trapping is allowed by the ON COM statement, a COM ON statement must have been executed. Once a COM ON statement has been executed, if a line number was specified in the ON COM statement, then BASIC will check every statement to see if characters have arrived from the communications line.

If the COM OFF statement was last executed, then communications trapping will not take place.

If the COM STOP statement has been executed, then no communications trapping can occur. However, any occurences of communications activity will be retained. This will result in an immediate trap upon execution of COM ON.

<table>
<tr><td></td><td>☐ Cassette</td></tr>
<tr><td># COMMON</td><td>■ Disk</td></tr>
<tr><td></td><td>■ Advanced</td></tr>
</table>

The Common statement passes the variables listed as its arguments to all CHAIN'ed programs.

Configuration

COMMON *variable* [*,variable*]

It is recommended that the Common statement appear at the beginning of a program. Any array variable included in a Common statement must be followed with parentheses ( ). If all variables are to be passed to the programs being CHAIN'ed, this can be accomplished by using the ALL option with CHAIN.

Example

100 COMMON A, B, C, D ( )

<table>
<tr><td></td><td>■ Cassette</td></tr>
<tr><td># CONT</td><td>■ Disk</td></tr>
<tr><td></td><td>■ Advanced</td></tr>
</table>

The Cont command is used to start program execution after execution has been stopped.

Configuration

CONT

Program execution may be stopped if the Ctrl-Break keys were pressed, if a Stop or End statement was executed, or if an error occurred. The Cont command will resume execution at the point where the program break occurred.

COS

■ Cassette
■ Disk
■ Advanced

The Cos function returns the cosine of its argument.

Configuration

$a = COS(b)$

Example

```
Ok
100  A = 4*COS(.6)
200  PRINT A
RUN
   3.30134246
Ok
```

CSNG

■ Cassette
■ Disk
■ Advanced

The CSNG function converts its argument to a single precision number.

Configuration

$a = CSNG(b)$

Example

```
Ok
100  X# = 963.3721422#
200  PRINT X#; CSNG(X#)
RUN
   963.3721422#      963.3721
Ok
```

CSRLIN

■ Cassette
■ Disk
■ Advanced

The CSRLIN variable returns the cursor's vertical coordinate.

Configuration

a = CSRLIN

The CSRLIN variable returns the current row position of the cursor on the active page (as explained in the SCREEN statement). The value returned will be between 1 and 25.

CVI, CVS, CVD

□ Cassette
■ Disk
■ Advanced

The CVI, CVS, and CVD functions are used to convert string variable types to numeric variable types.

Configuration

a = CVI(*2-byte string*)
a = CVS(*4-byte string*)
a = CVD(*8-byte string*)

CVI converts a 2-byte string to an integer. CVS converts a 4-byte string to a single-precision number, and CVD converts an 8-byte string to a double-precision number.

DATA

■ Cassette
■ Disk
■ Advanced

Data statements contain the numeric and string constants which later are accessed by Read statements.

Configuration

DATA *constant* [,*constant*]

Where;

constant   may be any numeric or string constant. Expressions are not allowed in a Data statement.

Numeric constants may be in integer, fixed point, floating point, hex, or octal format. String constants in Data statements need not be enclosed in quotation marks unless the string contains commas, colons, trailing blanks, or leading blanks.

An unlimited number of Data statements may be included in a program. As many constants as can be contained on a line can be included with a Data statement.

The constants included in the Data statements can be envisioned as one long list of items. The Read statements access the constants in the Data statements sequentially. The variable type in the Read statement must correspond with the constant being read from the Data statement. Otherwise, a "Syntax error" will occur.

DATE$

□ Cassette
■ Disk
■ Advanced

DATE$ is used to set or retrieve the date. It can be used as a variable or as a statement.

Configuration

$$a\$ = \text{DATE}\$ \qquad \text{variable}$$
$$\text{DATE}\$ = b\$ \qquad \text{statement}$$

When used as a variable in the following format:

$$a\$ = \text{DATE}\$$$

the current date is returned as a 10 character string in the form mm-dd-yyyy. The "mm" gives the month. The "dd" gives the day in the month, and the "yyyy" gives the year.

When used as a statement in the following format,

$$\text{DATE}\$ = b\$$$

the current date will be set to that given in $b\$$. $b\$$ can take any of the following forms:

```
mm-dd-yy
mm/dd/yy
mm-dd-yyyy
mm/dd/yyyy
```

The year must be between 1980 and 2099. If the month or day is entered as a single digit, a zero will be assumed to precede it. If only 2 digits are given for the year, these digits will be assumed to be preceded by 19.

Example

```
Ok
100  DATE$ = "7/15/82"
200  PRINT DATE$
RUN
  07-15-1982
Ok
```

DEF FN

■ Cassette
■ Disk
■ Advanced

The DEF FN statement is used to define a function written by the user.

Configuration

DEF FN*name* [(*argument*[,*argument*]...)] = *function definition*

Where;

name is a variable name, which when preceded by FN becomes the name of the function.

argument is an argument of the function being defined. The argument is a variable name in the function definition. When the function is called, the argument will be replaced with a value.

function definition are the statements which perform the function's operation.

Any *arguments* appearing in the *function definition* are used only to define the function. If a variable with the same name as an *argument* appears in the program, these variables will not be affected.

The function may return either a string or a numeric value depending upon the function type. The function type is given in *name* in the same way as variable types are defined. If the *function definition* does not return the type of data specified in the *name*, a "Type mismatch" error will occur.

The DEF FN statement must appear in a program prior to the point where it is called. If a function is called before it is defined, the following error will appear:

Undefined user function

Example

```
Ok
100  DEF FNTT(X) = SQR(X) + 1
200  X = 49
300  Y = FNTT(X)
400  PRINT Y
RUN
 7
Ok
```

DEFDBL, DEFSTR
DEFINT, DEFSNG,

■ Cassette
■ Disk
■ Advanced

These statements are used to declare variable types as integer, single-precision, double-precision, or string.

Configuration

$$ \text{DEF} \quad \begin{Bmatrix} \text{INT} \\ \text{SNG} \\ \text{DBL} \\ \text{STR} \end{Bmatrix} \quad alpha[-alpha]\ [,alpha[-alpha]]... $$

Where;

> *alpha* is a letter of the alphabet

The letter specified in the DEF statement will be the type of variable defined. However, if the variable appears with a type declaration character (%, !, #, or $), that will supercede the DEF statement.

If DEF statements are to be used, they must be executed before any variables being defined are encountered in the program.

Example

```
100  DEFINT A-D
200  DEFSTR E
300  DEFDBL F-M, Z
```

In line 100, the variables A through D are declared as integer variables. In line 200, the variable E is defined as a string variable. In line 300, the variables F through M and Z are defined as double precision variables. All other variables will be assumed to be single-precision.

DEF SEG

- ■ Cassette
- ■ Disk
- ■ Advanced

DEF SEG is used to define the current segment used for storage. A succeeding BLOAD, BSAVE, CALL, PEEK, POKE, VARPTR, or USR definition will define an actual physical address in memory as an offset into this segment.

Configuration

DEF SEG [= *address*]

Where;

   address is a number or numeric expression from 0 to 65535.

If the optional *address* is not included, the segment will be set to BASIC's Data Segment (DS), which is the beginning of the user work area in memory.

If an *address* is specified, that value should be predicated upon a 16 byte boundary. The value given in *address* is moved left 4 bits (times 16) to create the segment address to be used for any ensuing operation.

Example

100 DEF SEG = &HB800

DEF USR

■ Cassette
■ Disk
■ Advanced

DEF USR is used to give the starting address of a machine language subroutine which is to be called later by the USR function.

Configuration

DEF USR [*digit*] = *offset*

Where;

digit can be any digit from 0 to 9.

offset is an integer or integer expression from 0 to 65535.

Digit refers to the number of the USR routine for which an address is being specified. *Digit's* default value is 0.

The value given in *offset* is added to the current segment value to give the USR routine's starting address.

Example

```
100  DEF SEG = 0
200  DEF USR0 = 25000
```

DELETE

■ Cassette
■ Disk
■ Advanced

The Delete command is used to delete program lines.

Configuration

DELETE [*line*] [–*line*]

The *line* or range of lines specified will be erased. A period may be used in place of *line* to denote the current line. If a specified *line* does not exist, an "Illegal function call" error will result.

Example

DELETE 100——►line 100 is erased
DELETE 60-70——►lines 60 to 70 are erased
DELETE –20——►all lines up to and including 20 are erased.

DIM

■ Cassette
■ Disk
■ Advanced

DIM is used to initialize and reserve space in memory for arrays.

Configuration

DIM *variable(subscript)* [*,variable(subscript)*]

The DIM statement assigns a value of zero to all of the elements of numeric arrays and the null value to the elements of string arrays.

If an array variable name that was not defined with a DIM statement is used in a program, that array will be allowed a maximum subscript value of 10.

Example

DIM A(15), B(7)

DRAW

□ Cassette
□ Disk
■ Advanced

The Draw statement is used to draw an object specified by a string containing drawing commands. The Draw statement is only used in the graphics mode.

Configuration

DRAW *string*

Where;

   string is a string expression containing drawing commands.

We will discuss the movement commands first. These commands are described as follows:

U*n*	Move up.
D*n*	Move down.
L*n*	Move left.
R*n*	Move right.
E*n*	Move diagonally up and right.
F*n*	Move diagonally down and right.
G*n*	Move diagonally down and left.
H*n*	Move diagonally up and left.

Where;

   n gives the distance to be moved. The number of points to be moved is calculated by multiplying *n* times the scaling factor, which is set by the S command.

   M *x,y*   Move absolute or relative. If x is preceded by a plus (+) or minus (–) sign it is relative. If not, it is absolute.

The spacing of the horizontal, vertical, and diagonal points is **determined** by the aspect ratio of your screen. The standard **aspect** ratio is 4/3. This means that four horizontal points are the **same** length as three vertical points.

The movement commands can be preceded by the prefix commands, B and N. These are described below:

   B   Moves as indicated without the plotting of any points.

   N   Moves per the command but returns to the original position when the movement has been completed.

The following commands can also be used with DRAW:

   A*n*   This command sets an angle at the value indicated by *n*. *n* can be any value from 0 to 3, where 0 indicates 0 degrees, 1 indicates 90 degrees, 2 indicates 180 degrees, and 3 indicates 270 degrees.

Cn   This command sets the color to the value indicated by *n*. *n* can range from 0 to 3 in medium resolution or from 0 to 1 in high resolution.

Sn   This command is used to set the scale factor. *n* can range from 1 to 255. To calculate the scale factor, divide *n* by 4. The scale factor is multiplied by the distances given with the movement commands to determine the actual distance to be moved.

X *string* This command executes the substring. This allows the user to execute a second string from within the original string. The X command allows the user to define a part of a drawing as a separate part from the definition of the entire object.

With all of the commands, the argument *n* can either be a constant or it can be a variable. If *n* is a variable, it must be preceded by an equal sign (=). Also, a semicolon must be used to delimit commands where a variable is used for *n*.

Example

```
100  SCREEN 1
200  X = 30
300  DRAW "U=X; R=X;"
```

■ Cassette
■ Disk
■ Advanced

EDIT

The Edit command is used to display a line for editing purposes.

Configuration

EDIT *line*

Where;

line   is the line number of a line in the program. If the *line* specified does not exist, the following error message will appear;

Undefined line number

A period can be used for *line* if the user wishes to specify the current line. The Edit statement displays the specified line. The cursor is positioned at the beginning of the line number. The line may then be edited as described in Chapter 6.

END

■ Cassette
■ Disk
■ Advanced

The End statement is used to end program execution. The End command closes any open files and returns control to the command level.

Configuration

END

An End statement can be placed anywhere in the program.

Example

1000 IF X = Y THEN END ELSE GOTO 100

EOF

■ Cassette
■ Disk
■ Advanced

The EOF function is used to test for the end of file condition.

Configuration

a = EOF (filenumber)

Where;

filenumber is the number of the file as specified in the Open statement.

If the end of file has been reached, the EOF file will return a value of –1 (true). If the end of file has not been reached, the EOF file will return a value of 0.

Example

```
100  OPEN "TEXT.DAT" FOR INPUT AS #5
200  IF EOF(5) THEN 999
```

ERASE

■ Cassette
■ Disk
■ Advanced

The Erase statement is used to erase arrays from a program.

Configuration

ERASE *arrayname* [,*arrayname*]...

Where;

arrayname refers to the name of the array.

ERASE is often used when an array is to be redimensioned in a program. If the user attempts to redimension an array without it previously being ERASE'd, the following error message will be displayed;

Duplicate Definition

The Erase statement is also often used in situations where a program is running short of storage space. Once the arrays have been ERASE'd, the memory space previously allocated for arrays will be freed for use by the program.

Example

```
100  DIM A(10,10), B(5), C(7,5)
200  ERASE A(10,10)
300  DIM A(5,5)
```

ERR, ERL

- Cassette
- Disk
- Advanced

The ERR and ERL variables can be used to return the error code and the line number associated with that error.

Configuration

$$a = ERR$$
$$b = ERL$$

The ERR variable returns the error code for the last error. The ERL variable returns the line number of the line in the program where that error was discovered.

The ERL and ERR variables are often used in conjunction with an IF...THEN statement to test for an error condition as shown in the following example:

Example

```
100  ON ERROR GOTO 999
       .
       .
       .
999  IF ERR = 27 THEN LOCATE 1,1:
         PRINT "Please Turn on Printer";: RESUME
```

ERROR

■ Cassette
■ Disk
■ Advanced

The Error statement allows the user to duplicate a BASIC error. The Error statement can also be used to allow a user to define his own error codes.

Configuration

ERROR *n*

Where;

n   is an integer or integer expression from 0 to 255.

If the argument *n* specified with ERROR is the same as an error code used in BASIC, then the Error statement will duplicate that error's occurrence when it is executed. If an error routine had previously been defined with an On Error statement, then the error routine will be executed after that Error statement has been executed. If an error routine had not been previously defined, then the appropriate error message will be printed and program execution will stop.

If a value is used for *n* that is different than any of the error codes used by BASIC, then the user will have the opportunity to define his own error code. The newly-defined error code should have an error handling routine. If it does not, the following message will be printed:

Unprintable error

and program execution will stop.

Example

```
100  ON ERROR GOTO 999
200  INPUT "Keyin The Year";YEAR
300  IF YEAR<1982 OR YEAR>1999 THEN ERROR 200
       .
       .
       .
999  IF ERR = 200 THEN PRINT "INCORRECT ENTRY":
       IF ERL = 300 THEN RESUME 200
```

EXP

■ Cassette
■ Disk
■ Advanced

The EXP function is used to calculate the exponential function.

Configuration

$$a = EXP(b)$$

The value returned by the EXP function is the mathematical function e raised to the power specified by the argument b. The argument b must be less than or equal to 88.02969. Otherwise, the Overflow message will be displayed, infinity will be given as the value a, and program execution will continue.

Example

```
Ok
100  B = 4
200  PRINT EXP(B)
RUN
 54.598150
Ok
```

FIELD

□ Cassette
■ Disk
■ Advanced

The FIELD statement is used to reserve space for variables in a random file buffer.

Configuration

FIELD [#] *filenumber, width* AS *stringvariable*
[*,width* AS *stringvariable*]...

Where;

filenumber	is the number of the file. This was specified in the OPEN statement.
width	is a number or numeric expression which indicates the number of character positions which are to be allocated to *stringvariable*.
stringvariable	is a string variable which is used for random file access.

Field statements are used to enter data into a random buffer for a Put statement or to extract random data from a buffer after a Get statement has been executed. The Field statement does not actually place data into the random file buffer. This is performed by the LSET and RSET statements.

In the following example, the Field statement allocates the first 10 positions in the random file buffer for the string variable A$. The next 15 positions are reserved for the B$, and the following 30 positions are reserved for C$.

Example

FIELD 1, 10 AS A$, 15 AS B$, 30 AS C$

FILES

□ Cassette
■ Disk
■ Advanced

The Files command is used to display the filenames of the files contained on a diskette.

Configuration

FILES [*filespec*]

Where;

filespec   is a file specification

If the optional file specification is not included with the Files command, then all of the files on the current drive will be listed.

The filename match characters (? and *) may be used in the filename portion of the file specification. All files on the current drive that match the filename portion of the file specification will be listed.

Examples

FILES

FILES "*.DAT"

FILES "B:*.*"

In the first example, all of the files in the current drive will be listed. In the second example, all files on the current drive with an extension of .DAT will be listed. In the final example, all files on drive B will be listed.

FIX

■ Cassette
■ Disk
■ Advanced

The Fix function truncates its argument to an integer.

Configuration

$a = FIX(b)$

The Fix function deletes the decimal portion of its argument and returns only the integer portion. The Fix function differs from the INT function in that Fix does not return the next lower number when its argument is negative.

Example

```
Ok
PRINT FIX 67.345
 67
Ok
PRINT -63.99
 -63
Ok
```

FOR...NEXT

■ Cassette
■ Disk
■ Advanced

The FOR...NEXT statements are used to execute a sequence of statements a set number of times.

Configuration

FOR *variable* = *a* TO *b* STEP *c*
.
NEXT [*variable*] [,*variable*]

Where;

variable   is set to a single precision variable or an integer (*a*,*b*,*c*) and is used as a counter. *a* is the initial value of the counter, and *b* is the final value. The counter is incremented by the amount named after STEP (*c*). If a value is not given after STEP, it is assumed to be 1.

The program lines following the FOR statement are executed until the NEXT statement is encountered. At this point, the counter is incremented by the value specified after STEP. If no such value is specified, the counter will be increased by 1.

The value for the counter is then compared with its maximum value (*b*). As long as the counter's value is less than the final value, program control will branch back to the statement following the FOR statement. This entire process will then be repeated.

When the counter's value is greater than the specified maximum value (*b*), program execution will continue with the statement immediately following the NEXT statement. This will exit the FOR...NEXT loop.

One FOR...NEXT statement may be placed within another FOR...NEXT statement. This is known as **nesting.** When FOR...NEXT loops are nested, each FOR...NEXT loop must use a different variable name for the counter. Also, the NEXT statement for the inside loop must appear before the NEXT statement for the outside loop. However, if both loops end at the same point, a single NEXT statement may be used to end these. Be certain that the *variable* for the inside loop appears before that of the outside loop. A NEXT statement like the following,

```
NEXT A,B
```

would be interpreted as follows:

```
NEXT A
NEXT B
```

A NEXT statement can be used without a variable. In such a situation, the NEXT statement will be applied to the last FOR statement.

Example

```
Ok
100 B = 5
200 FOR A = 1 TO B
300 PRINT A;
400 NEXT
RUN
 1 2 3 4 5
Ok
```

FRE

The Fre function returns the number of "free" bytes in memory (ie those not being used).

Configuration

a = FRE(b)
a = FRE(b$)

The arguments used with FRE are dummy arguments. When FRE is used with a string argument, a **housekeeping** will be performed before the function returns the number of free bytes. A housekeeping is where BASIC gathers all useful data and frees any areas of memory which were once used for strings, but are currently unused.

Areas assigned to strings can become unused because strings in BASIC can have variable lengths. Every time a different value is assigned to a string variable, its length may change. This may cause the space assigned to a string to become partially unused. A housekeeping eliminates this unused space.

Whenever BASIC determines that the available work area in memory is being depleted, a housekeeping will be automatically undertaken.

Example

```
Ok
PRINT FRE(1)
 17397
Ok
```

GET

☐ Cassette
■ Disk
■ Advanced

The Get statement is used to read a record from a random file into a random buffer.

Configuration

GET [#] *filenumber* [,*number*]

Where;

filenumber   is the number assigned to the file when it was opened.

number   is the number of the record which is to be read.

If the optional parameter *number* is omitted, the next record following the last Get statement will be read into the buffer.

The Get statement can also be used with communications files. In these instances, the optional parameter *number* specifies the number of bytes to be read from the communications buffer.

Example

```
100 OPEN "A:VENDOR.DAT" AS #1
200 FIELD 1, 30 AS NAME$, 39 AS ADDR$, 35 AS CITY$
300 GET 1
400 PRINT NAME$, ADDR$, CITY$
```

GET (Graphics)

☐ Cassette
☐ Disk
■ Advanced

The Get statement is used in the graphics mode to read points from an area of the video screen.

Configuration

GET ($a1$, $b1$)-($a2$, $b2$), *arrayname*

Where;

$a1, b1$ & $a2, b2$ are used to specify a rectangle within which GET will read the colors of the points. This rectangle will have points ($a1, b1$) and ($a2, b2$) as opposite corners.

arrayname   is the name of an array which is used to hold the image. This array must be numeric, but it can be any precision. The required array size in bytes can be calculated with the following formula,

$$4 + INT((a*c+7)/8)*b$$

where a is the length of the horizontal side of the rectangle, b is the length of the vertical side, and c is 2 in medium resolution and 1 in high resolution.

If we applied this formula to a situation where the Get statement is to be used with a 12 by 12 image in medium resolution, the number of bytes required would be,

$$4 + INT((12*2+7)/8)*12$$

or, 40 bytes.

The number of bytes for each array element is as follows:

- integer ⟶ 2 bytes per element
- single precision ⟶ 4 bytes per element
- double precision ⟶ 8 bytes per element

In this situation, an integer array with at least 20 elements could be used.

GOSUB, RETURN

- Cassette
- Disk
- Advanced

The GOSUB, RETURN statements are used to branch to a subroutine and then return from it.

Configuration

GOSUB *line*
.
.
RETURN

A subroutine is called by the Gosub statement. When the Return statement is encountered within that subroutine, program control will branch back to the statement following the Gosub statement just executed.

Subroutines may appear at any point within the program. However, it is good programming practice to group all subroutines near the beginning of the program.

Example

```
Ok
 100 GOTO 600
 200 PRINT X
 300 Y=X*X
 400 PRINT Y
 500 RETURN
 600 X = 0
 700 FOR I = 1 TO 3
 800 X=X+1
 900 GOSUB 200
1000 NEXT
1100 END
RUN
 1
```

(output continued on next page)

```
1
2
4
3
9
Ok
```

GOTO

■ Cassette
■ Disk
■ Advanced

The GOTO statement is used to branch program control to another program line.

Configuration

GOTO *line*

The ON...GOTO statement allows the program to branch to a number of different lines depending upon the answer to the conditional expression.

Example

```
100  ON X GOTO 500,600,700,999
     .
     .
     .
999  END
```

HEX$

■ Cassette
■ Disk
■ Advanced

The HEX$ function returns a string which contains the hexadecimal equivalent of the function's argument (assumed to be decimal).

Configuration

a$ = HEX$(*b*)

The decimal argument (*b*) is rounded to an integer before the function is executed.

Example

```
Ok
100 INPUT A
200 A$ = HEX$(A)
300 PRINT "DECIMAL VALUE IS";A
400 PRINT "HEXADECIMAL VALUE IS";A$
RUN
 ?50
 DECIMAL VALUE IS 50
 HEXADECIMAL VALUE IS 32
```

IF

■ Cassette
■ Disk
■ Advanced

The IF statement sets a condition which will influence the program flow.

Configuration

IF *expression* [,] THEN *clause* [[,] ELSE *clause*]
IF *expression* GOTO *line* [[,] ELSE *clause*]

Where;

　clause　can be either a BASIC statement, a series of statements, or a line number.

In the first configuration, if the *expression* following the IF statement evaluates as true (not zero), the *clause* following the THEN statement will be executed. If the *expression* following the IF statement evaluates as false (zero), the *clause* following THEN will be disregarded, and the *clause* following the optional ELSE statement will be executed (if present). If an ELSE statement is not present, the program will proceed to the next line.

In the second configuration, if the *expression* following the IF statement evaluates as true, program control will branch to the *line* specified. If the *expression* evaluates as false, the statement will be ignored and the program will proceed to the next line.

Example

```
100 IF X=1 THEN Y=1 ELSE Y=2
200 IF Y=1 GOTO 999
     .
     .
999 END
```

INKEY$

■ Cassette
■ Disk
■ Advanced

INKEY$ is used to read a character from the keyboard.

Configuration

*a$* = INKEY$

The value returned by INKEY$ is a string consisting of either zero, one, or two characters. If no characters are waiting at the keyboard, then the null string will be returned. If a one character string is returned, that string will contain the character read from the keyboard. If a two character string is returned, an extended character code is being returned. The first character is hex 00, followed by the extended character code. The extended character codes are listed in Appendix E.

While the INKEY$ variable is being executed, characters will not be displayed on the screen. However, all characters will be transmitted to the program except for the following:

```
    Ctrl-Break ⟶ used to stop the program.
  Ctrl-Number ⟶ used to send the system into a writing state.
   Alt-Ctrl-Del ⟶ used to perform a system reset.
         Prtsc ⟶ used to print the screen.
```

One character returned by INKEY$ can be assigned to a string variable and used in conjunction with another BASIC statement to check for an operator entry.

Example

```
100  PRINT "Press any key to resume execution"
200  A$ = INKEY$
300  IF A$ = "  " GOTO 200
```

INP

■ Cassette
■ Disk
■ Advanced

INP returns the byte read from the port specified by its argument.

Configuration

$$a = INP(b)$$

Example

```
100  X = INP(255)
```

INPUT

■ Cassette
■ Disk
■ Advanced

The Input statement permits data entry while the program is being executed.

Configuration

INPUT [*"prompt"*;] *variable* [,*variable*]

Where;

prompt   is a string which is to be displayed on the console before data is accepted from the keyboard.

prompt is optional, and need not be included in the Input statement.

When an Input statement is executed, program execution will stop temporarily. A question mark will be displayed on the screen. If *prompt* was included in the Input statement, the prompt will be displayed in front of the question mark.

If you do not want the question mark prompt printed, you can eliminate this by using a comma rather than a semi-colon after INPUT.

After the Input statement has been executed, the user may enter the desired data at the keyboard. That data is assigned to the *variable(s)* listed in the Input statement. The number of data items input must equal the number of *variables* listed. Also, the type of data entered must agree with the type specified in *variable*. The data items must be delimited by commas when input.

If the operator enters the wrong number of data items, or the wrong type of data, the following error message will be displayed:

Redo from start

If data is to be entered for just one variable and you wish to enter a null value for a string variable or 0 for a numeric variable, you may do so by pressing Enter.

Example

```
Ok
100  INPUT "ENTER A NUMBER";A
200  PRINT "THE NUMBER ENTERED IS" A
300  END
RUN
 ENTER A NUMBER? 7.93
 THE NUMBER ENTERED IS 7.93
Ok
```

INPUT#

■ Cassette
■ Disk
■ Advanced

The Input# statement is used to read data items from a sequential file or device and to assign those items to program variables.

Configuration

INPUT# *filenumber, variable [,variable]...*

Where;

filenumber   is the number assigned to the file when it was OPEN'ed.

variable   is the name of the variable that will be assigned a data item from the file.

The data items being read and assigned to the *variable(s)* may either be from a sequential file on diskette or cassette, from a communications adapter, or from the keyboard.

With the Input# statement, a prompt (?) is not displayed as with Input.

Like the Input statement, the type of data being read from the file must agree with the *variable* type.

The data items should appear in the data file just as they would if they were being keyed in as a response to an Input prompt.

When numeric items are being read, any leading blank spaces, carriage returns, and line feeds will be disregarded. When a character is encountered that is neither of the above, this character will be regarded as the start of a number. When a blank space, a comma, line feed, or carriage return is encountered, the number will be assumed to have ended.

When string items are being read, again leading blank spaces, carriage returns, and line feeds will be disregarded. When a character is encountered that is neither of the above, this character will be regarded as the start of the string. If the first character is a quotation mark, the string will include all of the characters between that first quotation mark and the next. Note that a quotation mark should not appear within the string itself, as BASIC will interpret this as the end of the string.

If the first character of the string is not a quotation mark, the end of the string will be interpreted as the first comma, carriage return, or line feed encountered.

If the end of file is encountered when either a numeric or string item is being input, the entry of that item will be ended.

INPUT$

■ Cassette
■ Disk
■ Advanced

The Input$ function returns a string with a length specified in the function which is read from either the keyboard or from a file number specified in the function.

Configuration

$$a\$ = INPUT\$(b[, [\#]\ c])$$

Where;

     a$ is the string returned by the function.

     b is the number of characters to be returned.

     c is the optional file number.

If the keyboard is used for input, characters will not be displayed on the screen. Also, all control characters except Ctrl-Break will be passed through. Ctrl-Break is used to interrupt program execution. The user need not press the Enter key to end his response to INPUT$ when the entry is from the keyboard.

The Input$ function is preferred over Input# and Line Input# for use with communications files. The Input# is the least desirable method of data input from a communications file, as input stops when either a carriage return or comma is encountered. The Line Input# function stops when a carriage return is encountered. The Input$ function allows every character read to be included in the string. Because all ASCII characters may be significant in communications, INPUT$ is the preferred method when communications files are being used.

Example

```
100  PRINT "ENTER END TO EXIT"
200  A$ = INPUT$(3)
300  IF A$ = "END" GOTO 999
      .
      .
999  END
```

INSTR

■ Cassette
■ Disk
■ Advanced

The Instr function searches for the initial appearance of one string within another string. The position where the match occurs is returned by the function.

Configuration

$$a = INSTR([b,]\ c\$,\ d\$)$$

Where;

   a   is the value returned by the function.

   b   is an optional number or numeric expression from 1 to 255. *b* specifies the position within *d*$ where the search is to begin.

  c$ is the string to be searched. c$ may be a string variable, string expression, or string constant.

d$* is the string which is to be searched for. *d$ may be a string variable, string expression, or string constant.

Example

```
Ok
100  C$ = "ABCDEFG"
200  D$ = "C"
300  PRINT INSTR(C$,D$)
RUN
 3
Ok
```

INT

■ Cassette
■ Disk
■ Advanced

The Int function returns the integer value of its argument regardless of whether the argument is positive or negative. INT will return the largest integer which is less than or equal to the argument

Configuration

$$a = INT(b)$$

Example

```
Ok
PRINT INT(49.99)
 49
Ok
PRINT INT(-40.01)
 -41
Ok
```

KEY

- Cassette
- Disk
- Advanced

The Key statement is used to either set or display the soft keys.

The soft keys are initialized with the following values:

```
F1 = LIST              F6 = ,"LPT1:"  ⟨Enter⟩
F2 = RUN  ⟨Enter⟩       F7 = TRON  ⟨Enter⟩
F3 = LOAD"             F8 = TROFF  ⟨Enter⟩
F4 = SAVE"             F9 = KEY
F5 = CONT  ⟨Enter⟩      F10 = SCREEN 0,0,0  ⟨Enter⟩
```

The Key On statement lists the soft key assignments on the 25th line of the screen. If the screen width is 40, 5 of the 10 soft keys will be displayed. If the screen width is 80, all 10 of the soft keys will be displayed. In either the 40 or 80 column widths, the first six characters will be displayed.

The Key Off statement erases the display of the soft key assignments on the 25th line of the video display. The Key Off statement does not turn off the soft keys.

KEY LIST displays all 15 characters of all 10 soft keys on the screen.

The first configuration,

KEY *keynum, b$*

is used to assign the string *b$* to the key specified in *keynum*. *b$* may range from 1 to 15 characters. If *b$* is longer than 15 characters, only the first 15 will be recognized.

If a null string is assigned to a soft key, that key will be disabled.

When a soft key is pressed, one character is returned via the INKEY$ function every time the soft key is pressed. When a soft key is pressed that has previously been disabled, INKEY$ will return a two character string with the first character being binary zero and the second the key scan code. The key scan codes are given in Appendix E.

After a soft key has been reassigned, or after the last character has been received via INKEY$ from a soft key string, the following DEF SEG statement should be executed:

DEF SEG: POKE 106,0

This will help avoid problems with the input buffer.

Examples

```
100  KEY ON
200  KEY OFF
300  KEY 1, "LPRINT"
400  KEY 1, "  "
```

In the preceding example, program line 100 displays the soft keys in line 25 of the video screen. Line 200 turns off the display. In line 300, "LPRINT" is assigned to soft key 1. In line 400, function key 1 is disabled as a soft key.

KEY(a)

☐ Cassette
☐ Disk
■ Advanced

The Key(a) statement is used to specify a key which is to be trapped in a BASIC program.

Configuration

```
KEY(a) ON
KEY(a) OFF
KEY(a) STOP
```

Where;

a   is a number or numeric expression from 1 to 14. This number indicates the key which is to be trapped. The following numbers correspond with the keys to be trapped.

> 1-10   F1 to F10 function keys
> 11   Cursor Up
> 12   Cursor Left
> 13   Cursor Right
> 14   Cursor Down

The Key(a) On statement causes the function or cursor control key specified to be trapped. Once a key has been specified with the Key(a) On statement, BASIC will check to see if that key was pressed every time a statement is executed. If a line number is specified in an On Key(a) statement, BASIC will perform a GOSUB to the line number indicated if it senses that the key specified in KEY(a) ON was pressed.

The Key(a) Off statement deactivates the Key(a) On statement.

In the Key(a) Stop statement, no trapping of the specified key actually occurs. However, if the specified key is pressed, that event will be stored in memory. If a Key(a) On statement is executed for that key, a trap will occur immediately.

KILL

☐ Cassette
■ Disk
■ Advanced

The Kill command is used to delete the file specified from a diskette.

Configuration

KILL *filespec*

Where;

filespec   is a file specification. If the file includes a filename extension, that must be included in the *filespec* used with the Kill command.

If the device or drive specifier is not included in *filespec*, then the current disk drive will be assumed.

A file that is open cannot be KILL'ed. If a Kill command is executed for an open file, the following error will occur:

File already open

Example

100 KILL "A:TEXT.DAT"

LEFT$

■ Cassette
■ Disk
■ Advanced

The Left$ function returns the number of characters specified in the second expression of the argument to the leftmost of the string specified in the first part of the argument.

Configuration

$$a\$ = LEFT\$(b\$,x)$$

Where;
 a$ is the string returned by the function.
 b$ is the string searched by the function.
  x is the number of characters to be returned.

LEN

■ Cassette
■ Disk
■ Advanced

The Len function returns the length of the string specified in the expression.

Configuration

$$l = LEN(a\$)$$

Where;

 l is the length of the string
 a$ is the string

LET

■ Cassette
■ Disk
■ Advanced

The LET statement is an optional keyword often found in an assignment statement. An assignment statement is one that determines the value of an expression and then assigns that result to the variable named in the assignment statement.

Configuration

LET *variable* = *expression*

The *variable* must be of the same data type as the expression. For example, if *variable* is a string, *expression* must also be a string. If *variable* is an integer or real number, then *expression* must also be numeric.

Example

```
100 LET A$ = "JOHN"
200 Z = X + Y
```

LINE

■ Cassette
■ Disk
■ Advanced

The Line statement is used only in the graphics mode to draw a line or box on the screen.

Configuration

LINE [(*a1,b1*)] - (*a2,b2*) [,[*color*] [,B[F]]]

Where;

(*a1,b1*),(*a2,b2*)   are the coordinates

color   is the color number from 0 to 3. In medium resolution, *color* chooses the color from the current palette set by the Color statement. Color 0 will be used for the background color, and color 3 for the foreground. In high resolution, a *color* of 0 designates black, while a color of 1 indicates white.

B indicates box.

BF indicates filled box.

The Line statement can be used as follows to draw a line:

LINE (0,50) - (319,50)

The first set of coordinates specify the starting and ending coordinates. The foreground color will be used for the line as no value is given for *color*.

The Line statement can also be used to draw a line where no beginning coordinates are given:

LINE - (319,150)

In such a case, the last point referenced will be used as the starting point.

The color can be specified in the line statement as per the following,

LINE (0,0) - (50,100), 1

in which color 1 is specified.

The optional parameter B (for box) instructs BASIC to draw a rectangle with the points specified in (a1,b1),(a2,b2) as the opposite corners. When F (for filled box) is included with B, the interior points of the rectangle will be filled with the color indicated.

In the preceding example, the Line statement was used in absolute form. The Line statement can also be used in relative form. In relative form, the coordinates are given as follows,

LINE (150,150) - STEP(–50, –50)

Here, a line will be drawn from (150,150) to (100,100).

LINE INPUT

■ Cassette
■ Disk
■ Advanced

The Line Input statement is a variation of the Input statement. The Line Input statement allows an entire line (maximum of 254 characters) to be input to a string variable.

Configuration

LINE INPUT[;] ["*prompt*";] *variable$*

Where;

prompt is a prompt message that will be displayed on the screen before data can be input.

variable$ is the string variable that will accept the data being input.

Unlike the Input statement, a question mark will not be printed by the Line Input statement.

The data input after the prompt appears will be assigned to the string variable specified. When the user presses Enter, the entry will end.

If the optional semi-colon is included after LINE INPUT, a carriage return/line feed to the screen will not occur following the pressing of Enter.

LINE INPUT#

- Cassette
- Disk
- Advanced

The Line Input# statement is a variation of the Input statement. The Line Input# statement allows an entire line (maximum of 254 characters) to be input from a sequential file to a string variable.

Configuration

LINE INPUT# *filenumber, variable$*

Where;

filenumber   is the number assigned to a file when it was opened.

variable$ is the string variable that will accept the data being input.

The Line Input# statement will read all of the characters (up to 254) until a carriage return is encountered.

The Line Input# statement is often used in instances where each line in a file has been separated into different fields. LINE INPUT# is also used in situations where a BASIC program saved in ASCII code is read as data by another program.

Example

```
100 OPEN "VENDOR" FOR OUTPUT AS #1
200 LINE INPUT "Vendor data?";INFO$
300 PRINT #1, INFO$
400 CLOSE 1
500 OPEN "VENDOR" FOR INPUT AS #1
600 LINE INPUT #1, INFO$
700 PRINT INFO$
800 CLOSE 1
RUN
     Vendor data? JOHN SMITH 1 MAIN ST. VILLE, IL
```

JOHN SMITH 1 MAIN ST. VILLE, IL
Ok

LIST

■ Cassette
■ Disk
■ Advanced

The List command is used to list the program stored in memory on the video display or another device.

Configuration

LIST [*line*[-[*line*]]] [,*filespec*]

Where;

> *line*   is a line number.

> *filespec*   is the file specification.

If *filespec* is not included in the List command, the *line* indicated will be sent to the screen. If the range given by *lines* is omitted, then the entire program will be listed.

When a dash (-) is used with lines, the following possibilities are available.

1. If only the first *line* is specified, only that line number and any higher line numbers will be listed.

2. If only the second *line* is specified, all of the program lines from the beginning of the program through the *line* named are listed.

3. If both *lines* are included, that range will be listed.

A period (.) can be used to indicate the current line.

Listings being sent to the screen by default can be stopped by pressing Ctrl-Break. Listings being sent to a specified device cannot be terminated with Ctrl-Break.

Examples

```
LIST
LIST 20, "LPT1:"
LIST 100-200
LIST 50-100, "B:SUB1.BAS"
```

In the first example, the whole program is listed to the screen. In the second, line 20 is listed on the printer. In the third example, lines 100 to 200 are listed to the screen. In the final example, lines 50 through 100 are listed to a file named SUB1.BAS in drive B.

LLIST

■ Cassette
■ Disk
■ Advanced

LLIST is used to list all or part of the program held in memory to the printer (LPT1:).

Configuration

LLIST [*line*[-[*line*]]]

Where;

line   is a line number.

The use of the *line* ranges for LLIST functions exactly like LIST.

To stop LLIST, you must turn the printer off for 10 seconds. Ctrl-Break will not terminate LLIST.

Example

```
LLIST
LLIST 100
LLIST 110-120
```

LLIST 130-
LLIST -100

In the first example, LLIST will print a listing of the whole program. In the second, line 100 will be listed on the printer. In the third example, lines 110 through 120 will be listed on the printer. In the fourth example, all lines from 130 to the end of the program will be listed on the printer. In the final example, all lines from the beginning of the program through line 100 are listed.

LOAD

■ Cassette
■ Disk
■ Advanced

The Load command is used to load a program from the device specified into memory. When the R option is specified, the program will execute after it is loaded.

Configuration

LOAD *filespec* [,R]

Where;

    filespec   is the file specification.

If you are using Cassette BASIC, CAS1: is the only device that can be used. If no device is given in *filespec*, CAS1: is the default device.

If you enter the Load statement in the direct mode, the filenames on the cassette tape will be displayed on the screen followed by a period and a single letter. These letters indicate the type of file and are as follows:

B   for BASIC program created with the Save command (in internal format).

P   for BASIC programs which are protected (created with the Save, P command).

A for BASIC programs in ASCII format (created with the SAVE,A command).

M for memory image files created with the BSAVE command.

D for data files created by OPEN followed by output statements.

The filenames on the cassette will be displayed one by one. If the file encountered does not match that named in *filespec,* the following message will be displayed:

Skipped

If the file on the cassette matches that in *filespec,* the following message will be displayed:

Found

The Load command can be aborted by pressing Ctrl-Break. If this occurs, the search will stop for the named file and BASIC will return to the direct mode.

When the Load command is executed within a BASIC program, the filenames are not displayed on the video display.

If the Load command is executed when using Disk or Advanced BASIC, a filename extension of .BAS is assumed if none is given. Also, the current drive will be assumed if no device is given in *filespec.*

Example

LOAD "MENU", R

□ Cassette
■ Disk
■ Advanced

LOC

The Loc function returns the current position within the file specified. With a random file, LOC returns the record number of the last number read from or written to that file. With a sequential file, LOC returns the number of records read from or written to the file since it was opened.

Configuration

$$a = LOC(filenumber)$$

Where;

filenumber   is the number assigned to the file when it was opened.

When LOC is used with a communications file, the function returns the number of characters in the input file waiting to be read.

Example

```
100  IF LOC(1)>100 THEN GOTO 999
     .
     .
999 END
```

LOCATE

■ Cassette
■ Disk
■ Advanced

The Locate statement is used to position the cursor on the screen.

Configuration

LOCATE [*row*] [,[*column*] [,[*cursor*] [,[*start*] [,*stop*]]]]

Where;

row   is the line number on the screen (1-25)

column   is the column number on the screen (1-40 or 1-80).

cursor is a value which indicates whether the cursor is on or off (0 indicates off, 1 indicates on).

start is the starting scan line (0-31).

stop is the ending scan line (0-31).

Once the cursor is positioned with the Locate statement, any succeeding input or output statements to the screen will initially send characters to the position specified by LOCATE.

The optional *start* and *stop* parameters allow the user to regulate the size of the cursor. The size is specified via scan lines. The scan line at the top of the character position is 0. The bottom scan line is 7 when the Color/Graphics Monitor Adapter is installed; 13 with the IBM Monochrome Display and Printer Adapter. If the *start* scan line is specified and *stop* is not, the *stop* will take on the value used for *start*. If *start* is greater than *stop*, then a two part cursor will extend from the bottom line back to the top.

Usually, line 25 on the video display is reserved for messages. However, by using the KEY OFF statement, the user can turn off the soft key display. The Locate function can then be used as follows to place information in line 25:

LOCATE 25,1:PRINT...

Example

100 LOCATE 1,1

LOF

□ Cassette
■ Disk
■ Advanced

The LOF function (length of file) returns the number of bytes which were allotted for a file.

Configuration (Diskette Files)

$$a = \text{LOF}(filenumber)$$

Where;

filenumber is the number assigned to the file when it was opened.

When LOF is used with diskette files, the value returned by the function will be a multiple of 128. For example, if the actual number of bytes contained in a file were 244, the number returned by LOF would be 256 (128 x 2).

LOF can also be used in communications to return the amount of free space in the input buffer.

Example

$$A = \text{LOF}(1)$$

LOG

- Cassette
- Disk
- Advanced

The Log function returns the natural logarithm of its argument.

Configuration

$$a = \text{LOG}(b)$$

Example

```
Ok
PRINT LOG(15)
 2.708050
Ok
```

LPOS

■ Cassette
■ Disk
■ Advanced

LPOS returns as its argument, the position of the printhead within the printer buffer. This is not necessarily the physical position of the printhead on the printer.

Configuration

$$a = LPOS(b)$$

In Cassette BASIC, b is a dummy argument. In Disk and Advanced BASIC, b specifies which printer is to be tested. The following are used:

0 or 1	LPT1:
2	LPT2:
3	LPT3:

Example

100 IF LPOS(1)>80 GOTO 900

LPRINT

■ Cassette
■ Disk
■ Advanced

LPRINT is used to print data to the printer.

Configuration

LPRINT [*data*] [,]...

Where;

data   includes the string or numeric expressions to be printed. These may be separated by either commas or semi-colons.

The LPRINT statement functions exactly like PRINT except that it sends data to the printer. LPRINT assumes the printer width to be 80 characters. This value may be changed with a WIDTH "LPT1:" statement.

Example

```
Ok
100 FOR I = 1 TO 3
200 LPRINT "CUSTOMER";I
300 NEXT I
RUN
  CUSTOMER 1
  CUSTOMER 2
  CUSTOMER 3
```

LPRINT USING

■ Cassette
■ Disk
■ Advanced

LPRINT USING is used to print data at the printer.

Configuration

LPRINT USING *format$; data* [,]

Where;

format$ is a string constant or string variable which consists of special formatting characters. These are described in the PRINT USING statement section.

data   includes the string or numeric expressions to be printed. These may be separated by either commas or semi-colons.

The LPRINT USING statement functions exactly like PRINT USING except that it sends data to the printer. LPRINT assumes

the printer width to be 80 characters. This value may be changed
with a WIDTH "LPT1:" statement.

Example

```
Ok
LPRINT USING "##.##";.59
 0.59
Ok
```

LSET, RSET

□ Cassette
■ Disk
■ Advanced

LSET and RSET are used to move data from memory to a random
file buffer. LSET and RSET are generally used prior to a Put
statement.

Configuration

LSET *variable$* = *x$*
RSET *variable$* = *x$*

Where;

   variable$ is a string variable to be used for random file access.

In some cases, the string returned by LSET or RSET (*x$*), will need
a fewer number of bytes than the amount reserved by the Field
statement. In these situations, RSET will right-justify that string
and LSET will left-justify it. Blank spaces will be used to fill the
excess positions.

If *x$* is longer than the space reserved by FIELD, then the extra
characters are deleted from the right.

Numeric values must be first converted to strings via the MKI$, MKS$, or MKD$ functions before they can be used with LSET or RSET.

Example

100 RSET Z$ = MKS$(TOTAL)

MERGE

■ Cassette
■ Disk
■ Advanced

The Merge statement is used to merge program lines from an ASCII program file to the program currently held in memory.

Configuration

MERGE *filespec*

Where;

filespec   is the file specification.

When the Merge statement is executed, the device specified will be searched for the file specified. In Cassette BASIC, the default value for device is CAS1: (The only device allowed with the Merge statement in Cassette BASIC). In Disk and Advanced BASIC, the default for the device name is the current drive.

When the specified file is located, the program lines in that file will be merged with the program in memory. If any of the lines in the file specified in the Merge statement have the same line number as lines in the program in memory, the lines from the file being merged will replace those in memory.

Once the Merge statement has finished executing, the resulting file will be held in memory, and program control will return to command level.

The program being merged must have been saved in ASCII

format. This is accomplished by using the Save command with the A option. If the file being merged was not saved in ASCII format, the following error will occur,

Bad file made

and the program in memory will not be altered.

Example

MERGE "B:PROGRAM2.BAS"

MID$

■ Cassette
■ Disk
■ Advanced

When used as a function, MID$ returns a part of a string as specified by its arguments. When used as a statement, MID$ will replace a part of one string with another string.

Configuration (Function)

$$a\$ = MID\$(b\$, c\ [,d])$$

Where;

a$ is the string returned by the function.

b$ is the string from which a$ is being returned.

c is the beginning character in b$ from which a$ is to be returned.

d is the number of characters to be returned in a$ from b$. If d is not included, all characters to the right of c will be returned.

Configuration (Statement)

$$MID\$\ (b\$, c\ [,d]) = a\$$$

When used as a statement, MID$ replaces the characters in *b$* with those in *a$*, beginning at position *c*. The optional value *d* gives the number of characters from *a$* which will be used. If *d* is not included all of *a$* will be used.

When MID$ is used as a statement to replace characters in *b$*, the length of *b$* will not change. For example, if *b$* consists of seven characters and *a$* consists of nine characters, the length of *b$* will remain at seven characters.

Example (Function)

```
Ok
100  A$ = "ANNETTE"
200  PRINT MID$(A$,3,3)
RUN
 NET
Ok
```

Example

```
Ok
100  A$ = "PHILADELPHIA"
200  MID$(A$,6,7) = "NTHROPY"
300  PRINT A$
RUN
 PHILANTHROPY
Ok
```

MKI$, MKS$, MKD$

☐ Cassette
■ Disk
■ Advanced

MKI$, MKS$, and MKD$ are used to convert numeric values to string values.

Configuration

```
a$ = MKI$(integer)
a$ = MKS$(single precision)
a$ = MKD$(double precision)
```

Where;

> a$ is the string value returned by the function.
>
> *integer*   is an integer or an expression that evaluates to an integer.
>
> *single precision*   is a single precision number or an expression that evaluates to a single precision number.
>
> *double precision*   is a double precision number or one that evaluates to a double precision number.

MKI$ converts an integer to a 2-byte string. MKS$ converts a single precision number to a 4-byte string. MKD$ converts a double precision number to an 8-byte string.

MKI$, MKS$, and MKD$ are often used to convert numeric values to string values before placing them in a random file buffer with LSET or RSET.

Example

```
100  TOTAL = X.TOT + Y.TOT
200  FIELD #1, 4 AS TOTAL$
300  LSET TOTAL$ = MKS$(TOTAL)
400  PUT #1
```

MOTOR

■ Cassette
■ Disk
■ Advanced

The Motor statement is used to turn on or turn off the cassette player from within a program.

Configuration

MOTOR [*condition*]

Where;

condition is a value which determines whether the motor will be on or off. A value of zero for *condition* turns off the motor. A non-zero value turns it on. If no *condition* is given, the motor will be switched to its opposite state. That is, if the motor was on, it will be off, and vice versa.

NAME

☐ Cassette
■ Disk
■ Advanced

The Name command is used to change a diskette file's name.

Configuration

NAME *filespec* AS *filename*

Where;

filespec is the file specification of the file whose name is to be changed.

filename is the new filename.

In the following example, a file named TEXT.DAT on drive B will be renamed as FILE1.DAT.

Example

100 NAME "B:TEXT.DAT" AS "FILE1.DAT"

NEW

■ Cassette
■ Disk
■ Advanced

The New command erases the program currently stored in memory and clears all variables.

Configuration

NEW

The New command is usually executed to free memory space before a new program is entered. All files will be closed when the New command is executed. After the New command has been executed, program control will return to the command level.

OCT$

■ Cassette
■ Disk
■ Advanced

OCT$ is a function which returns the octal value of its argument (which is in decimal).

Configuration

a$ = OCT$(*b*)

Where;

b is the decimal argument. *b* is converted to an integer before conversion to octal is effected.

Example

```
Ok
PRINT OCT$(32)
 40
Ok
```

ON COM

□ Cassette
□ Disk
■ Advanced

The On Com statement is used to set up a line number which is to be trapped by BASIC when data is transmitted into the communications buffer.

Configuration

ON COM(a) GOSUB *line*

Where;

a   is the number identifying the communications adapter (1 or 2).

line   is the line number where a GOSUB will execute to if any characters have come into the communications buffer. If zero is used for *line*, the trapping of communications activity will be discontinued.

Before an On Com statement can be executed, a Com On statement must have been previously executed for the same communications adapter (specified in *n*). Once a Com On statement has been executed and if a non-zero line number was used in On Com, the BASIC will check the communications adapter named before executing every statement to see if any data has been received. If so, a GOSUB will be executed to the *line* given.

If a Com Off statement had been executed, no trapping will occur for the adapter.

If a Com Stop statement had been executed, no trapping will occur for the adapter. However, unlike the Com Off statement, if a character is received by the adapter, this event is remembered. When a Com On statement is executed, an immediate trap will occur.

When a character is received while the Com On and On Com statements are executing, and program control branches to a subroutine, a Com Stop statement is executed to prevent additional data being received from causing additional traps.

When a Return statement is executed in the subroutine, a Com On statement will be automatically executed.

It is not a good idea to use the communications trap for single character messages. In these situations with high baud rates, the trapping and reading of every single character may result in an overflow of the interrupt buffer for communications.

Generally, the communications trap routine is used to read an entire message from the communications line.

Example

```
100  ON COM(1) GOSUB 900
      .
      .
900  REM COMMUNICATIONS ROUTINE
      .
      .
950  RETURN
```

ON ERROR

■ Cassette
■ Disk
■ Advanced

The On Error statement allows errors to be trapped and transfers program control to an error handling routine.

Configuration

ON ERROR GOTO *line*

Where;

line   is a program line number

Once the On Error statement has been effected, when an error is detected, program control will branch to the specified *line*.

To disable error trapping, use zero (0) for *line*. Any future errors will result in the error code being printed and program execution being stopped.

If an On Error statement with a line of zero (0) is used in the error routine itself, execution will stop and the error message for the error causing the trap will be printed.

It is good programming practice to include the following,

ON ERROR GOTO 0

in error trapping routines where there is no recovery procedure for that error. As discussed previously, the error message for that error will print.

Error trapping does not occur within the error handling subroutines themselves.

Example

200 ON ERROR GOTO 900
  .
  .
900 IF ERR = 27 THEN PRINT "Turn on the printer":RESUME

ON...GOSUB, ON...GOTO

■ Cassette
■ Disk
■ Advanced

The On...Gosub and On...Goto statements are used to branch program control to one of several line numbers depending on the value appearing after ON.

Configuration

ON *a* GOTO *line* [,*line*]...
ON *a* GOSUB *line* [,*line*]...

The value of *a* controls which *line* is to be branched to. For instance, if *a* evaluates to 1, program control will branch to the line number given in the first *line*. If *a* evaluates to 2, program control will branch to the second *line*, etc...

If the On...Gosub statement is being used, the line number specified in *line* must be that of a subroutine. In other words, a Return statement eventually will have to be executed to return program control to the main routine.

If *a* evaluates to zero or to a number greater than the number of *lines* specified after GOTO or GOSUB, then the program will continue with the next executable statement.

Example

100 ON X GOSUB 200, 300, 400

ON KEY

□ Cassette
□ Disk
■ Advanced

The On Key statement specifies the line number of a subroutine to be branched to when the specified control or function key is pressed.

Configuration

ON KEY (a) GOSUB *line*

Where;

a is a number or numeric expression between 1 and 14 which indicates the key which when pressed will cause the branch in program control. These keys are as follows:

        1-10 Function keys F1 through F10
          11 Cursor Up
          12 Cursor Left
          13 Cursor Right
          14 Cursor Left

A Key On statement must have been executed prior to the On Key statement. Once Key On has been executed, an On Key statement can be executed. This will result in BASIC checking to see if the function key specified in On Key was pressed before the execution of every statement. If that key was pressed, a GOSUB to the indicated line will be executed.

If a Key Off statement is executed, the On Key statement will no longer have any effect.

If a Key Stop statement was executed, the key specified in On Key will not cause a branch to the indicated subroutine. However, if that key is pressed, the event will be remembered. If a Key On statement is subsequently executed, a branch to the *line* indicated in On Key will be immediately executed.

If the key specified in On Key is pressed while the Key On is on, a Key Stop will be executed. This will prevent the pressing of the specified key a second time from having any immediate effect. Once the Return statement in the subroutine has been executed, the Key On statement will be executed as well.

Example

100 ON KEY(7) GOSUB 900

ON PEN

□ Cassette
□ Disk
■ Advanced

The On Pen statement transfers control to a specified subroutine when the light pen is activated.

Configuration

ON PEN GOSUB *line*

Where;

line   is the line number of the subroutine to be branched to. If a *line* of 0 is specified, the On Pen statement will have no effect.

A Pen On statement must have been executed for the On Pen statement to have an effect. If a Pen On statement has been executed, BASIC will check to see if the light pen was turned on before it executes every statement. If so, the On Pen statement will execute a GOSUB to the *line* indicated.

If the Pen Off statement has been executed, then the On Pen statement will have no effect.

If a Pen Stop statement had been executed, then the occurrence of turning on the light pen will be remembered. When a Pen On statement is executed, a GOSUB to the *line* specified in the On Pen statement will be executed.

When the pen is turned on with the Pen On statement in effect, a Pen Stop statement will be executed immediately. Once a Return statement in the subroutine being branched to is executed, a Pen On will be executed.

Example

100 ON PEN GOSUB 900

ON STRIG

☐ Cassette
☐ Disk
■ Advanced

The On Strig statement specifies the line of a subroutine to be branched to if one of the joysticks is pressed.

Configuration

ON STRIG (a) GOSUB *line*

Where;

a   is 0 for the first joystick and 2 for the second.

line   is the line number of the subroutine to be branched to. If 0 is specified for *line*, the On Strig statement will be disabled.

A Strig On statement for the joystick indicated must have been executed for the On Strig statement to execute. If so, BASIC will check to see if the specified joystick had been pressed before executing each new statement. If it has, a GOSUB to the *line* indicated will be executed.

If a Strig Off statement had been executed, then pressing the joystick will have no effect.

If a Strig Stop statement had been executed, then pressing the joystick button will not have an immediate effect. However, if the joystick is pressed, that event will be remembered. If a Strig On statement is later executed, a branch to the indicated *line* will be effected.

If a joystick is pressed with Strig On and On Strig executing, a Strig Stop statement will be immediately executed. This prevents any further pressing of the joystick from having an immediate effect. However, if a Return statement is executed in the subroutine a Strig On statement will be executed.

Example

100 ON STRIG GOSUB 900

OPEN

■ Cassette
■ Disk
■ Advanced

The Open statement allows input and output to the specified file.

Configuration

OPEN *filespec* [FOR *mode*] AS [#] *filenumber* [LEN = *rcdlength*]

Where;

filespec   is the file specification.

mode   can be any one of the following:

INPUT for sequential input mode.

OUTPUT for sequential output mode.

APPEND for sequential output mode where the file is positioned to the end of the data file when that file is opened. If the specified file does not exist, the

APPEND causes that file to be created for the sequential output mode and positioned to its beginning. APPEND may only be used with diskette files.

In cases when *mode* is not included, random access will be assumed.

filenumber is an integer or integer expression with a value between 1 and the maximum allowable number of files. In Cassette BASIC, this maximum is 4. In Disk and Advanced BASIC, this maximum is 3, however it can be altered with the IF: option in the BASIC command. *filenumber* is used in subsequent statements and commands for file identification purposes.

rcdlength is an integer or integer expression which initializes the record length for random files. *rcdlength* has no effect on sequential files, and may range from 1 to 32676. However, *rcdlength* may not be greater than the number specified in the IS: option in the BASIC command. The default value for *rcdlength* is 128 bytes.

Configuration 2

OPEN *altmode,* [#] *filenumber, filespec* [*,rcdlength*]

Where;

altmode is a string or string expression with one of the following as its first character.

    O   indicates sequential output mode.

    I   indicates sequential input mode.

    R   indicates random input/output mode.

The Open statement reserves an input/output buffer for a file or device. The Open statement also specifies the mode of access to that buffer.

An Open statement must have been executed for a file or device before any input/output statements can be executed for that device. These include the following:

GET	PRINT#
INPUT$	PRINT USING#
INPUT#	PUT
LINE INPUT#	WRITE#

In IBM BASIC, the same file may be open under more than one file number. This allows the same file to be open under differing modes of access.

In Cassette BASIC, the default value for the device is CAS1:. In Disk or Advanced BASIC, the current drive is the default value for the device.

Example

```
100 OPEN "TEXT.DAT" FOR INPUT AS #1
200 OPEN "O", #1, "FILEA"
```

OPEN COM

☐ Cassette
■ Disk
■ Advanced

The Open Com statement is used to open a communications file.

Configuration

OPEN "COMa: [*speed*] [,*parity*] [,*data*] [,*stop*]"
AS [#] *filenumber*

Where;

    a indicates the number of the communications adapter (1 or 2).

speed   is an integer constant which indicates the transmit/receive rate in bits per second (bps). *Speeds* that can be used include 75, 110, 150, 300, 600, 1200, 1800, 2400, 4800, and 9600. The default value is 300 bps.

parity   is a one character constant which specifies the parity for transmitting and receiving. These are as follows:

        S   for SPACE. The parity bit is transmitted and received as the space (0) bit.

        O   for ODD. Odd transmit and odd receive parity checking.

        M   for MARK. The parity bit is transmitted and received as a mark (1 bit).

        E   for EVEN. Even is used for transmission parity, and even receive parity checking.

        N   for NONE. No transmit parity, and no receive parity checking.

The default value is EVEN (E).

data   is an integer constant which specifies the number of transmit/receive data bits. The following values can be used:

$$4, 5, 6, 7, \text{and } 8$$

The default value is 7.

stop   is an integer constant that specifies the number of stop bits. Either 1 or 2 are valid. The default values are as follows:

$$2 \longrightarrow 75 \text{ and } 110 \text{ bps}$$
$$1 \longrightarrow \text{for all others}$$

filenumber   is an integer or integer expression that indicates a valid file number.

The Open Com statement reserves a buffer for input and output to communications files. The Open Com statement allows RS232 asynchronous communication with other computers and peripherals. A communications device may only be open to one file number at any one time.

If 8 data bits are indicated, parity N must be specified. If 4 data bits are indicated, a parity other than N must be specified. When numeric data is being transmitted or received, 8 data bits must be specified.

Example

100 OPEN "COM1:1200, N, 8" AS #2

OPTION BASE

■ Cassette
■ Disk
■ Advanced

The Option Base statement is used to specify a minimum value for array subscripts.

Configuration

OPTION BASE a

Where;

a   is a default base of 1 or 0. The default for OPTION BASE is 0.

Example

100 OPTION BASE 1

OUT

■ Cassette
■ Disk
■ Advanced

The Out statement is used to send a byte to a machine output port.

Configuration

OUT *a*, *b*

Where;

    a   is the port number
    b   is the data to be transmitted.

The Out statement is used to adjust the video output. In the following example, the display will be shifted 5 characters to the right (assuming an 80 column width).

Example

OUT 980,2: OUT 981,85

PAINT

☐ Cassette
☐ Disk
■ Advanced

The Paint statement is used in the graphics mode of Advanced BASIC to place color in a specified area of the screen.

Configuration

PAINT (*a*,*b*) [, *color* [, *boundary color*]]

Where;

    (a,b)   are the coordinates of a point within the area to be colored in. These coordinates may be specified in absolute or relative form.

    color   is the color to be used (0 to 3).

    boundary   is the color of the edges of the form to be colored in (0 to 3).

The figure with edges of the boundary color is filled in with the *color* specified.

The (a,b) coordinates for PAINT must be inside the form to be PAINT'ed. If the optional *paint* is not included, the foreground color will be used.

If a complex form is to be PAINT'ed, a large amount of stack space may be required by the Paint statement. It may be a good idea in such applications to execute a Clear command at the beginning of the program to increase the amount of available stack space.

Example

```
100  SCREEN 1
200  LINE (0,0) - (70,70), 2, B
300  PAINT (50,50), 1, 2
```

PEEK

■ Cassette
■ Disk
■ Advanced

The Peek function will return the byte read from the memory location specified as its argument.

Configuration

$$a = PEEK(b)$$

Where;

a   is the value returned by the function. *a* must be an integer from 0 to 255.

b   is the offset from the current segment as defined in the Def Seg statement.

Example

```
100  IF PEEK(&H50) = 0 THEN GOSUB 900
```

PEN

The Pen statement and function are used to read the light pen.

Configurations

PEN ON
PEN OFF
PEN STOP
$a = \text{PEN}(b)$

Where;
a   is the integer returned by PEN.
b   is a number or numeric constant which returns an integer from 0 to 9. These are as follows:

0   a flag which specifies whether the pen was down since the last pull (–1 indicates down; 0 indicates not down).

1   gives the x coordinate where the pen was last utilized. X can range from 0 to 319 in medium resolution and from 0 to 639 in high resolution.

2   gives the y coordinate where the pen was last utilized. Y can range from 0 to 199.

3   gives the current pen switch value (–1 indicates down; 0 indicates up).

4   gives the last known valid x coordinate.

5   gives the last known valid y coordinate.

6   gives the character row position where the pen was last utilized (1 to 24).

7   gives the character column position where the pen was last utilized (1 to 40 or 1 to 80).

8   gives the last known valid character row (1 to 24).

9   gives the last known valid character column position (1 to 40 or 1 to 80).

The Pen On statement must be executed for the PEN read function to be used. Initially, the Pen function is off. Therefore, a Pen On statement must be executed before Pen read functions can be executed.

As explained in the On Pen statement section, the Pen On statement must be executed for trapping to occur with the On Pen statement.

The Pen Stop statement is only used in Advanced BASIC. The Pen Stop statement remembers light pen activity so that the event is immediately trapped upon execution of a subsequent Pen On statement.

Example

```
100 PEN ON
200 X = PEN(2)
300 PRINT X
400 PEN OFF
500 END
```

■ Cassette
■ Disk
■ Advanced

PLAY

The Play statement is used to play music.

Configuration

PLAY *music$*

Where;

music$ is a string constant or string expression consisting of music commands. These are as follows:

$$A\text{-}G \begin{Bmatrix} \# \\ + \\ - \end{Bmatrix}$$ The note given is played. # or + after the note means sharp, while – means flat.

Lx
This is used to set the length of each note. L1 means a whole note; L2 is a half note; L4 a quarter note; L16 a sixteenth note, etc... x may range from 1 to 64.

If you wish to change the length for only one note, you can do so by placing the length directly after the letter for the note (ex. A4 would be a quarter note A).

MF
This causes music to run in the foreground. Each note or sound will not begin to play until the preceeding note or sound has finished playing. MF (music foreground) is the default value.

MB
This causes music to play in the background. Each note or sound is placed in a buffer. This allows the BASIC program to continue execution as music plays in the background. As many as 32 notes can be played in the background at any one time.

MN
or music normal, results in every note being played at 7/8th of the value given in L (length).

ML
or music legato. This causes each note to be played at the entire length specified in L.

MS
or music staccato. This causes each note to be played at ¾ of the time specified in L.

Na
is used to play the note specified in a, where a can range from 0 to 84. Since there are 7 octaves available, there are 84 notes available. If a is 0, a rest is indicated.

Ob
is used to set the current octave. Seven octaves are available. These are numbered

from 0 to 6. Each octave extends from C to B. Octave 3 begins with middle C.

Pc is used to indicate a pause. The length of the pause (as given in c), may range from 1 to 64 and is calculated as in L (length).

Td is used to indicate the tempo. Tempo is defined by the number of quarter notes per second. d may range from 32 to 255. The default value for d is 120.

X string causes execution of the specified string.

a period following a note causes it to be played as a dotted note (the note's length is multiplied by 1.5). More than one period may follow a note. If more than one period does follow a note, it's length will be adjusted as indicated. For instance, 'A..." will play 3.37 times as long as "A". Periods may also follow a pause to lengthen it in the same manner.

Example

```
100  A$ = "B#B–D"
150  B$ = "O2XA$"
200  PLAY "P8XA$; XB$; XA$;"
```

POINT

■ Cassette
■ Disk
■ Advanced

The Point function returns the color of the point on the screen indicated as its argument. The Point function is only used in the graphics mode.

Configuration

$$c = POINT(a,b)$$

Where;

c   is the color value returned by the function.

a,b   are the coordinates of the point to be used as the argument.

If the point specified is out of range, the value returned is –1.

Example

100 IF POINT(100,100) = 1 THEN GOTO 900

POKE

- Cassette
- Disk
- Advanced

The Poke statement is used to write a byte to a specified address in memory.

Configuration

POKE a,b

Where;

a   is an address memory in the range of 0 to 65535. a is given as an offset from the current segment as given in the Def Seg segment.

b   is the data to be written to the memory location specified in a. b can range from 0 to 255.

Example

100 POKE 200,13

POS

■ Cassette
■ Disk
■ Advanced

The Pos function returns the present column position of the cursor.

Configuration

$$a = POS(b)$$

Where;

a   is the cursor column position.

b   is a dummy argument.

Example

100 IF POS(0)>40 THEN PRINT CHR$(13)

PRINT

■ Cassette
■ Disk
■ Advanced

The Print statement is used to display data on the screen.

Configuration

PRINT [*expressions*] [;]
? [*expressions*] [;]

If the optional *expressions* is omitted, a blank line will be displayed on the video screen. If *expressions* are included, these will be displayed on the screen. These *expressions* may be either numeric or string.

The position on the screen where each item is displayed is determined by the punctuation mark used to separate the items in *expressions*. Each display line is divided into print zones of 14 spaces each. A comma causes the next item encountered in *expressions* to be printed at the beginning of the next print zone.

A semi-colon causes the next item to be printed immediately following the preceding value. If one or more blank spaces is used to separate the items in *expressions,* the effect will be the same as using a semi-colon.

If the last item in *expressions* is ended with a semi-colon, the next Print statement will begin printing on the same line as the last Print statement immediately following the last item.

If a comma is used to end the list of items in *expressions,* the next Print statement will again print on the same line. However, that item will be printed at the next print zone.

If neither a comma nor a semi-colon ends the items in *expressions,* a carriage return will be executed before the next item is printed.

When numbers are PRINT'ed to the screen, they are always followed by a blank space.

Example

```
Ok
100  A$ = "ABC"
200  B$ = "DEF"
300  C = 5
400  PRINT A$; B$, C, C
500  END
RUN
 ABCDEF          5          5
Ok
```

PRINT USING

■ Cassette
■ Disk
■ Advanced

The Print Using statement is used to print string or numeric data in a pre-defined format.

Configuration

PRINT USING *format$*; *expressions* [;]

Where;

format$ is a string constant or variable consisting of the formatting characters.

expressions   consist of the string or numeric items that are to be printed. Each item in *expressions* must be separated with commas or semi-colons.

The formatting characters determine the manner in which the string or numeric data specified will be printed. The string formatting characters are as follows:

!   specifies that only the first character in the string is to be printed.

\ \   is used to specify the number of characters to be printed from the string. This number is the number of characters enclosed within the slashes plus 2. If the back-slashes are given with no spaces, then two characters will be printed. If the string is longer than the space allowed by the format, the extra characters will be dropped. If the field specified by the format is larger than the string, spaces will be added to the right of the string.

&   specifies a variable length string. When the format field is specified with &, the string will be output in the same manner as it is input.

The numeric formatting characters are as follows:

specifies a digit position. If the number being printed has fewer digits than allowed for by the formatting characters, that number will be right-justified in the formatting field.

.   A decimal point may be inserted anywhere in the format field.

+   A plus sign can be included at the beginning or end of the format string. This formatting character causes the number's sign (+ or –) to be printed in front of or behind the number.

–   The minus sign, when included at the end of the format string, will cause negative numbers to be printed with a trailing minus sign.

**   When placed at the beginning of a format field, a double asterisk causes any leading blanks in a numeric field to be filled with asterisks. These positions indicated by ** will be filled with digits if no blank spaces are available.

$$ The double dollar sign results in a dollar sign being printed at the left of the numeric field. The double dollar sign indicates two digit positions, one of which is a position for the dollar sign. Negative numbers cannot be used in a format with $$ unless they appear at the right of the number.

**$ The **$ formatting character combination causes a dollar sign to be printed before the number and any leading blanks to be filled with asterisks. **$ allows for 3 additional digit positions, one of which is the dollar sign.

,.   When a comma appears to the left of the decimal point in a numeric formatting string, the result is that a comma will be printed to the left of every third digit on the left hand side of the decimal point. A comma allows for an additional digit position.

^^^^   When four carats are placed after the formatting characters which indicate the digits, an exponential format is specified. These four carats allow for the printing of one of the following:

$$E \pm xx$$
$$D \pm xx$$

where x signifies a number.

— The underline character, when used in the format string, causes the next character to be printed as a literal character.

% A percent character is printed in front of a number when that number is larger than its format field. Also, if rounding causes a number to go beyond its format field, a percent sign will be printed in front of the rounded number.

Examples (String)

```
Ok
100  A$ = "JOHN": B$ = "MARY"
200  PRINT USING "!"; A$; B$
300  PRINT USING "  \ \  "; A$; B$
400  PRINT USING "&"; B$
RUN
 JM
 JOMA
 MARY
Ok
```

Examples (Numeric)

```
Ok
PRINT USING "##.##"; 9.1, 19.7, 73.777, .337
 9.10      19.70      73.78       0.34
Ok
PRINT USING "+ ##.##"; 42.7, -.7, 7.9, 14.2
 +42.7      -.70      +7.90      +14.20
Ok
PRINT USING "##.##-"; -6.19, 27.331, -49.0
 6.19-      27.33      49.00-
```

```
Ok
PRINT USING "**##.##"; 117.229, -22.90, 1013.42
  *117.23       *-22.90        1013.42
Ok
PRINT USING "$$##.##"; 7.89, 12.99, 149.89
  $7.89        $12.99        $149.89
Ok
PRINT USING "**$##.##; 7.89, 12.99, 149.89, 1982.62
  ***$7.98       **$12.99       *$149.89       $1987.62
Ok
PRINT USING "#.##^^^^"; 489.1, .887, 149
  4.89E+02        8.87E-01        1.49E+02
Ok
PRINT USING "_##.#"; 7.9
  #7.9
Ok
PRINT USING "##.##"; 511.11
  %511.11
```

PRINT#, PRINT# USING

■ Cassette
■ Disk
■ Advanced

The Print# and Print# Using statements are used to write data to a file sequentially.

Configuration

PRINT# *filenumber,* [USING *format$;*] *expressions*

Where;

filenumber   is the number assigned to the file when it was opened.

format$ is a string constant or expression consisting of special formatting characters. These were explained in the section on the Print Using statement.

expressions   is one or more numeric and/or string items that are to be written to the file specified.

When sending data to a file via a Print# or Print# Using statement, the user must be careful to properly delimit the data items. Both numeric and string items in *expressions* must be delimited by a semi-colon as shown below:

PRINT #1, X; Y; Z
PRINT #1, X$; Y$; Z$

Using only the semi-colon as a delimiter can lead to problems when the data written to the file via PRINT# or PRINT# USING is read back from the file. For example, if X$ = "JOHN", Y$ = "SAM", and Z$ = "BILL", the following would be written to the specified file:

JOHNSAMBILL

Obviously, additional delimiters (known as explicit delimiters) must be inserted into the PRINT# statement as strings. This is shown below:

PRINT #1, X$; ", "; Y$; ", "; Z$

The preceding example would write the following to the specified file.

JOHN, SAM, BILL

This data can be read back from the file into 3 string variables.

If the strings being written contain commas, semi-colons, significant leading blanks, carriage returns, or line feeds, these characters should be written to the file surrounded by quotation marks given as a CHR$ function (CHR$ (34)).

For example, if A$ = "JOHN, SAM" and B$ = "BILL", the following statement,

PRINT #1, A$; ", "; B$

would write the following data to the file:

JOHN, SAM, BILL

If the following statement were executed,

INPUT #1, A$, B$

"JOHN" would be input into A$, and "SAM" would be input into B$. By separating the strings with double quotes (CHR$(34)) as shown below,

PRINT #1, CHR$(34); A$; CHR$(34); CHR$(34); B$; CHR(34)

the following would be written to the file:

"JOHN, SAM""BILL"

When the following statement is executed,

INPUT #1, A$, B$

"JOHN,SAM" would be input to A$, and "BILL" would be input to B$.

The Print# statement can also be used with the optional reserved word Using to print data to the file in a format specified by a format string. Format strings and formatting characters are discussed in the section on the Print Using statement.

PSET & PRESET

- Cassette
- Disk
- Advanced

PSET and PRESET are only used in the graphics mode. These statements are used to draw a point at a given screen location.

Configuration

PSET (a,b) [,color]
PRESET (a,b) [,color]

Where;

a,b   are the screen coordinates of the point to be set. These may be specified in either absolute or relative form.

color   is the color to be used (0 to 3). If the optional *color* is not included in the PSET statement, the foreground color will be used (3 in medium resolution; 1 in high resolution). If *color* is not specified in PRESET, the background color (0) will be used. If *color* is specified, PRESET and PSET work in an identical fashion.

Example

300 PSET (100,100), 2

PUT (Files)

□ Cassette
■ Disk
■ Advanced

The Put statement is used to write a record from a random buffer to a random file.

Configuration

PUT [#] *filenumber* [*,rcdnumber*]

Where;

filenumber   is the number assigned to the file when it was opened.

rcdnumber   is the record number of the record to be written. If *rcdnumber* is not included, the next available record (after the last PUT) will be used. When PUT is used with communications files, *rcdnumber* is used to designate the number of bytes to be written to the communications file.

Example

500 PUT #1, X%

PUT (Graphics)

The following configuration of the Put statement is used only in the graphics mode to write colors to a specified area on the screen.

Configuration

PUT *(a1,b1) array [,operation]*

Where;

a1,b1   are the coordinates of the top left hand corner of the area to be transferred.

array   stands for a numeric array which contains the data to be transferred.

operation   stands for one of the following:

    PSET
    PRESET
    XOR (The default value)
    OR
    AND

The Put statement when used in the graphics mode takes data out of the specified *array* and places in onto the video screen.

The optional *operation* provides a means whereby the data being transferred can be used in conjunction with existing data to gain some sort of special effect.

If PSET is used as the *operation,* the data from the *array* is stored on the screen. PRESET functions like PSET except that it forms a negative image.

AND is sometimes used as the *operation* in cases where an image is already in place beneath the image to be transferred. AND is used to transfer the image only.

OR is used to overlay the image specified in PUT over an image already in place.

XOR is used for animation purposes. When used with XOR the Put statement can be used to move an object over a background without erasing it.

When used in medium resolution, the And, Xor, and Or statements will affect the colors as outlined in Table 7-2.

Table 7-2. AND, XOR, OR Effects On Color

Array Color Value

AND	0	1	2	3
0	0	0	0	0
1	0	1	0	1
2	0	0	2	2
3	0	1	2	3

Screen Color Value (rows of AND table)

Array Color Value

OR	0	1	2	3
0	0	1	2	3
1	1	1	3	3
2	2	3	2	3
3	3	3	3	3

Screen Color Value (rows of OR table)

Array Color Value

XOR	0	1	2	3
0	0	1	2	3
1	1	0	3	2
2	2	3	0	1
3	3	2	1	0

Screen Color Value

RANDOMIZE

- Cassette
- Disk
- Advanced

The Randomize statement is used to reset the seed of the random number generator.

Configuration

RANDOMIZE [a]

Where;

a   is the new seed. If *a* is omitted, the user will be prompted to enter the new seed.

READ

- Cassette
- Disk
- Advanced

The Read statement is used to read items from the Data statement and assign these items to the variables specified in the Read statement.

Configuration

READ *variable* [, *variable*]

Where;

variable   may be either numeric or string. The *variable* type must agree with the data type being read.

Read statements are always used in combination with Data statements. The items in the Data statement are assigned to the *variables* given in the Read statement one by one. If the number of *variables* in the Read statement is greater than the number of items available in the Data statement, the following error will occur:

Out of data

If the number of *variables* given in the Read statement are fewer than the number of data items given in the Data statement, any future Read statements will begin reading at the first item which had not been previously read. If there are no more Read statements, these extra data lines will be ignored.

By executing a Restore statement, the data items will be read into the Read variables beginning with the first data item once again.

Example

```
100  DATA "MIAMI", "FLORIDA", 33507
200  READ CITY$
300  READ STATE$
400  READ ZIP.CODE
500  PRINT CITY$, STATE$, ZIP.CODE
RUN
  MIAMI          FLORIDA          33507
```

■ Cassette
■ Disk
■ Advanced

REM

The Rem statement is used to include programmer's remarks in the program listing. These remarks are generally used to detail the program's operation.

Configuration

REM *remark*

Where;

remark   can be any sequence of characters

Remarks may also be included at the end of a line by placing a single quote mark (') in front of the *remark* rather than the Rem statement.

Whenever a *remark* is placed on the same line with other BASIC statements, the *remark* must be the final statement on the line.

Remark statements are not executed. However, they are output just as they were entered when the program is listed. Remark statements cause execution to be slowed somewhat as they use available memory.

A Goto or Gosub statement can branch directly to a Rem statement. In these cases, program execution will continue with the next executable statement following the Rem statement.

Example

```
100  REM Calculate Future Value
200  I = 10 'Set interest rate to 10%
```

RENUM

■ Cassette
■ Disk
■ Advanced

The Renum command is used to renumber a program's line numbers.

Configuration

RENUM [*new#*] [*,old#*] [*,value*]

Where;

new# is the first new line number to be used in the re-numbering process. The default value for *new#* is 10.

old# is the line in the program where renumbering is to begin. The default is the program's first line.

value is the amount to be added or subtracted from the present new line number to generate the next new line number. The default for *value* is 10.

The Renum command will also change any references to a line number that has been changed. These references could be present in Goto, Gosub, On...Goto, On...Gosub, Erl, Then, and Else statements.

Example

RENUM 100, 500, 50

RESET

□ Cassette
■ Disk
■ Advanced

The Reset command is used to close all diskette files and reset the system buffer.

Configuration

RESET

RESTORE

■ Cassette
■ Disk
■ Advanced

The Restore statement resets the Data statement pointer to the line specified.

Configuration

RESTORE [*line*]

Where;

> *line* is a line number in the program containing a Data statement.

If a RESTORE is executed without a *line* being given, the next Read statement executed will read the first data item in the first Data statement in the program. If a *line* is given with the Restore statement, the next Read statement will read the first data item in the Data statement named in *line*.

Example

```
Ok
100  DATA 29, 39, 49, 59, 69, 79
200  READ A,B,C
300  READ D,E
400  RESTORE
500  READ F
600  PRINT A, B, C, D, E, F
RUN
 29    39    49    59    69    29
Ok
```

RESUME

■ Cassette
■ Disk
■ Advanced

The Resume statement is used to continue program execution after an error recovery routine was executed.

Configuration

RESUME [0]
RESUME NEXT
RESUME *line*

Where;

>line   refers to a program line number.

When RESUME [0] is used, program execution will continue at the program statement which caused the error. When RESUME NEXT is used, execution will continue at the statement directly after the statement causing the error. When RESUME *line* is used, execution will continue at the specified line number.

If a Resume statement is used in an area other than an error trap routine, the following error mesage will be printed:

>RESUME without error

Example

    100 ON ERROR GOTO 999
       .
       .
    999 IF ERR = 71 THEN PRINT "INSERT DISKETTE":
         RESUME 200

RETURN

■ Cassette
■ Disk
■ Advanced

When the Return statement is executed, program execution will resume with the statement following the most recently executed Gosub statement.

Configuration

>RETURN [*line*]

Where;

line   is a program line number. The use of *line* in a Return statement is only allowed in Advanced BASIC. This option allows the user to transfer program control to a specified line number while eliminating the Gosub entry. This option is generally used in event trapping routines.

Example

```
100  ON Y GOSUB 300, 400, 500
      .
      .
300  REM SUBROUTINE #1
      .
      .
399  RETURN
400  REM SUBROUTINE #2
      .
      .
499  RETURN
500  REM SUBROUTINE #3
      .
      .
599  RETURN
```

RIGHT$

■ Cassette
■ Disk
■ Advanced

The Right$ function returns the rightmost characters of a string specified as its argument. The number of characters returned is also given in the argument.

Configuration

$$a\$ = RIGHT\$ \ (b\$,c)$$

Where;

a$ is the string returned by the function.

b$ is the string from which the characters are to be returned.

c   is the number of characters to be returned. If c is zero, the null string is returned. If c is greater than or equal to the length of the string given in *b$*, then that entire string will be returned.

Example

```
Ok
100 B$ = "SAN FRANCISCO, CALIFORNIA"
200 PRINT RIGHT$(B$,10)
RUN
 CALIFORNIA
Ok
```

RND

■ Cassette
■ Disk
■ Advanced

RND is used to return a random number between 0 and 1.

Configuration

$$a = RND[(b)]$$

Where;

a   is the random number generated.

b   is used to reseed the random number generator when *b* is given as a negative value. If *b* is positive or is left out, RND(*b*) will generate the next random number in the sequence.

RND(0) repeats the last number generated.

The same series of random numbers will be generated unless a new seed is specified for the random number generator. This can be accomplished via the Randomize statement or by using a negative value for *b*, as described earlier.

Example

```
Ok
100 FOR I = 1 TO 3
200 PRINT RND(I);
300 NEXT
RUN
 .7291626      .1425771      .7301725
Ok
```

RUN

The Run command is used to begin program execution.

Configuration

RUN [*line*]
RUN *filespec* [,R]

Where;

line is a program line number. If *line* is included, execution will begin with that line number. If *line* is not specified, execution will begin with the lowest line number.

filespec is a file specification.

In the first configuration, the Run command will execute the program currently held in memory.

In the second configuration, the file given in *filespec* is loaded from a cassette or diskette into memory and run. The current memory contents will be erased before the program to be run is loaded. Also, all open files are closed unless the R option is included. If so, all data files will remain open.

Example

```
Ok
100 PRINT "This is being run."
RUN
 This is being run.
Ok
```

SAVE

■ Cassette
■ Disk
■ Advanced

The Save command is used to save a BASIC program file on diskette or cassette.

Configuration

SAVE *filespec* [,A]
SAVE *filespec* [,P]

Where;

filespec   is the file specification for the file to be saved.

The program file named in *filespec* is written to the device indicated. For diskette files, if the filename consists of 8 characters or less and a filename extension is not given, the filename extension .BAS is automatically added to the filename.

If a file already exists on the diskette with the same filename as that of the program file to be saved, the file to be saved will be written over the existing file.

CAS1: is the default device name in Cassette BASIC. In fact, in Cassette BASIC, CAS1: is the only allowable device. The default device is the current drive for Disk and Advanced BASIC.

If the optional A is included in the Save command, the program will be saved in ASCII format. If A is not included, the file will be saved in compressed binary format.

The P (or Protection) option causes the program to be saved in an encoded binary format. A protected program cannot be used with the LIST or EDIT commands.

Example

SAVE "A:NEW", A

SCREEN Function

■ Cassette
■ Disk
■ Advanced

The Screen function will return the ASCII code for the character displayed at the screen location given in the function.

Configuration

a = SCREEN (*row, column* [*,b*])

Where;

a is the ASCII code returned by the function.

row is a number or numeric expression corresponding to the row (1 to 25) on the screen.

column is a number or numeric expression corresponding to the column (1 to 40 or 1 to 80) on the screen.

b is a number or numeric expression which evaluates to a value of true (non-zero) or false (zero). If b is included and evaluates to true, the color attribute for the character will be returned instead of its ASCII code. The values returned for the color attribute may range from 0 to 255, and can be interpretted as follows:

(a MOD 16) will be the foreground color.

(a MOD 128) will return the background color.

a >127 will evaluate as true (−1) if the character is blinking; false (0) if not.

Example

```
100 A = SCREEN (100,100)
200 B = SCREEN (100,100,1)
```

SCREEN Statement

■ Cassette
■ Disk
■ Advanced

The Screen statement is used to set the screen attributes which are to be used by any subsequent statements.

Configuration

SCREEN [*mode*] [,[*colorenable*] [,[*activepg*] [,*visualpg*]]]

Where;

mode   is a number or numeric expression which will evaluate to an integer value of 0, 1, or 2. 0 indicates the text mode at the current width (40 or 80). 1 indicates the medium resolution graphics mode (320 x 200). 2 indicates the high resolution graphics mode. 1 and 2 are only available with the Color/Graphics Monitor Adapter.

colorenable   is a numeric expression which returns a value of true or false. *colorenable* enables the color. In the text mode, a false value for *colorenable* disables color allowing only black and white. A true value enables color. In the medium resolution graphics mode, a true value for *colorenable* will disable color, while a false value will enable color. *colorenable* has no effect in high resolution as the only colors allowed are black and white.

activepg   or active page. This can be a number or numeric expression evaluating to an integer from 0 to 7 for screens with a width of 40, or from 0 to 3 for screens with a width of 80. *activepg* selects the page which is to be written to by output statements to the screen.

visualpg   or visual page. The ranges for *visualpg* are the same as for *activepg*. *visualpg* selects the page to be displayed on the screen.

Any of these parameters may be omitted from the Screen statement. If this is the case, the parameter omitted will keep its old value.

If the new screen mode matches that of the previous mode, the screen won't be changed. However, if the new screen mode differs from the old, the new screen mode will be stored and the old screen mode will be erased. The foreground color will be set to white and the border to black.

Example

100 SCREEN 0,1,0,0

SGN

- Cassette
- Disk
- Advanced

SGN returns the sign of its argument.

Configuration

$a = SGN(b)$

If the argument b is positive, SGN returns a value of 1. If b is zero, SGN returns a value of 0. If b is negative, SGN returns a value of −1.

Example

100 ON SGN(A) + 2 GOTO 100,200,300

SIN

- Cassette
- Disk
- Advanced

The Sin function is used to calculate the sine of its argument.

Configuration

$a = SIN(b)$

Where;

b is an angle in radians.

Example

```
Ok
PRINT SIN(1.7)
 .9916648
Ok
```

SOUND

■ Cassette
■ Disk
■ Advanced

The Sound statement is used to transmit sounds from the PC's speaker.

Configuration

SOUND *frequency, ticks*

Where;

frequency is the frequency desired in cycles per second (Hertz). *frequency* may range from 37 to 32707.

ticks is the length of the sound in clock ticks. There are 18.2 clock ticks per second. *ticks* may range from 0 to 15535.

When the Sound statement is used to produce a sound, the program continues execution until another Sound statement is executed. The current Sound statement can be turned off by executing another Sound statement with a *ticks* of zero. If the current Sound statement is not turned off in this manner, it will continue to execute, and no new Sound statements will be executed until the first Sound statement has been completed.

Example

```
100 REM Create Sounds
200 SOUND 100,2
```

SPACE$

■ Cassette
■ Disk
■ Advanced

The Space$ function returns a string consisting of the number of blank spaces given as the function's argument.

Configuration

a$ = SPACE$(*b*)

Example

```
Ok
100  FOR X = 1 TO 3
200  A$ = SPACE$(X)
300  PRINT A$;X
400  NEXT
RUN
 1
  2
   3
Ok
```

SPC

■ Cassette
■ Disk
■ Advanced

SPC is used to print the number of spaces given as its argument.

Configuration

PRINT SPC(a)

Where;

    a   is the number of spaces (0 to 255)

SPC can only be used in conjunction with Print, Lprint, and Print# statements.

Example

```
Ok
100  PRINT SPC(10) "JOHN" SPC(10) "CLARK"
RUN
        JOHN        CLARK
Ok
```

SQR

■ Cassette
■ Disk
■ Advanced

SQR returns the square root of its argument.

Configuration

$$a = SQR(b)$$

Example

```
Ok
100  X = 49
200  PRINT SQR(X)
RUN
 7
Ok
```

STICK

■ Cassette
■ Disk
■ Advanced

The Stick function returns the X and Y coordinates of the two joysticks.

Configuration

$$a = STICK(b)$$

Where;

b may range from 0 to 3 and will return the coordinate listed below:

0   Returns the X coordinate for joystick A.

1   Returns the Y coordinate for joystick A.

2   Returns the X coordinate for joystick B.

3   Returns the Y coordinate for joystick B.

Example

100 X = STICK(2): Y = STICK(3)

STOP

■ Cassette
■ Disk
■ Advanced

The Stop statement is used to end program execution and return program control to the command level.

Configuration

STOP

When a Stop statement is executed, the following message will be displayed,

Break in xxxxx

where xxxxx is the line number where the Stop statement was executed.

The Stop statement differs from the End statement in that it does not close open files.

If a Cont command is executed following a Stop command, program execution will continue.

Example

```
100 INPUT X,Y
200 Z = X + Y
300 STOP
400 A = Z * 4
500 PRINT A
RUN
?4,8
Break in 300
Ok
PRINT Z
 12
Ok
Cont
 48
Ok
```

STR$

■ Cassette
■ Disk
■ Advanced

STR$ returns the string representation of its argument.

Configuration

a$ = STR$(a)

In the following example, A$ would consist of the string "40". In this case, "40" is a string--not a number. In other words, "40" (in its string equivalent) would not be used in calculations.

Example

```
100  A$ = STR$(40)
```

STRIG

STRIG returns the status of the joystick buttons.

Configuration

STRIG ON
STRIG OFF
a = STRIG(b)

Where;

a is the value returned by the function.

b is a number or numeric expression between 0 and 3. The values returned for b are as follows:

0   a value of –1 is returned if the button for joystick A was pressed since the execution of the last STRIG(0) statement. If not, a value of 0 is returned.

1   A value of –1 is returned if the button for joystick A is currently being pressed, and 0 if not.

2   A value of –1 is returned if the button for joystick B was pressed since the execution of the last STRIG(2) statement, and 0 if not.

3   A value of –1 is returned if the button for joystick B is currently pressed, and 0 if not.

A STRIG ON must have been executed before any form of the STRIG(b) function can be executed. Once STRIG ON has been executed, BASIC will check to see if a joystick button had been pressed before beginning a new statement.

STRIG( )

☐ Cassette
☐ Disk
■ Advanced

STRIG( ) is used to enable or disable trapping of the joystick buttons by ON STRIG.

Configuration

STRIG(a) ON
STRIG(a) OFF
STRIG(a) STOP

Where;

a   is a number or numeric expression that evaluates to 0 or 2. 0 represents joystick A, and 2 represents joystick B.

STRIG ON must be in effect before the pressing of a joystick button can be trapped by ON STRIG. Once STRIG ON has been executed, a check will be made by BASIC at the beginning of every statement to determine whether or not a joystick button had been pressed.

If STRIG OFF is executed, no trapping of the pressing of a joystick button will take place.

If STRIG STOP is executed, trapping of the pressing of a joystick button does not occur. However, if a button is pressed, that event will be stored in memory. When a STRIG ON is executed, an immediate trap will take place.

STRING$

■ Cassette
■ Disk
■ Advanced

The String$ function prints a string of the length specified in its argument. All of the characters returned by the String$ function will either be the character corresponding to the ASCII code specified in its argument, or the first character in the string specified in its argument.

Configuration

a$ = STRING$(*b*,*c*)——→*c* is ASCII code
a$ = STRING$(*b*,*c*$)——→ *c*$ is string

Example

```
Ok
100  A$ = STRING$(5,61):PRINT A$
RUN
 = = = = =
Ok
100  B$ = "JOHN"
200  C$ = STRING$(5,B$)
300  PRINT C$
RUN
 JJJJJ
Ok
```

SWAP

■ Cassette
■ Disk
■ Advanced

The Swap statement is used to exchange values between two variables.

Configuration

SWAP *variable 1, variable 2*

Be careful that you do not use the Swap statement with variables storing different data types (ex. A% and A$). If the Swap statement is used with variables of different types, the following error will occur:

Type mismatch

Example

```
Ok
100 A$ = "JOHN": B$ = "JACK"
200 PRINT A$, B$
300 SWAP A$, B$
400 PRINT A$, B$
RUN
 JOHN      JACK
 JACK      JOHN
Ok
```

SYSTEM

□ Cassette
□ Disk
■ Advanced

The system command is used to return to DOS from BASIC. All files are closed by the System command prior to the return to DOS.

TAB

■ Cassette
■ Disk
■ Advanced

The Tab function is used to move the print position (on screen or line printer) to that indicated in its argument.

Configuration

```
PRINT TAB(a)
LPRINT TAB(a)
```

Where;

a   is the position to which the print position is to be moved. If the current print position on a line is already beyond *a*, then TAB will move the print position to that specified by *a* on the next line.

The first position (to the left) is position 1. The position farthest to the right can be calculated by subtracting 1 from the value specified in WIDTH.

Example

```
Ok
100 PRINT "FIRST NAME" TAB(25) "LAST NAME"
200 PRINT "JOHN" TAB(25) "JOHNSON"
RUN
 FIRST NAME               LAST NAME
 JOHN                     JOHNSON
```

TAN

■ Cassette
■ Disk
■ Advanced

The Tan function returns the tangent of its argument.

Configuration

$$a = TAN(b)$$

Where;

b   is the angle in radians. Degrees can be converted to radians by multiplying by PI/180 where PI = 3.141593.

Example

```
Ok
100  A = TAN(35*3.141593/180)
200  PRINT A
RUN
 .7002076
Ok
```

TIME$

□ Cassette
■ Disk
■ Advanced

TIME$ can be used as a statement to set the current time. TIME$ can also be used as a variable to obtain the current time.

Configuration (Statement)

$$TIME\$ = a\$$$

Configuration (Variable)

$$a\$ = TIME\$$$

Where;

a$ is a string expression or constant containing the current time value.

When TIME$ is used as a statement to set the current time, a$ may be specified in any of the following three formats:

hh   where *hh* sets the hour (0 to 23). The minutes and seconds will be set at 00 by default.

hh:mm   will set the hours and minutes. The range for minutes is 0 to 59. The seconds will be set to 00 by default.

hh:mm:ss will set the hours, minutes, and seconds. The range for seconds is 0 to 59.

When TIME$ is used to obtain the current time, that time will be returned as an 8 character string in the form *hh:mm:ss* where *hh* specifies hours in the range of 00 to 23, *mm* specifies minutes in the range of 00 to 59, and *ss* specifies seconds in the range of 00 to 59.

Example

```
Ok
100  A$ = TIME$
200  PRINT A$
RUN
 11:52:57
Ok
```

TRON & TROFF

■ Cassette
■ Disk
■ Advanced

The Tron and Troff commands are used to trace the execution of program statements.

Configuration

TRON
TROFF

The Tron (Trace On) command sets a trace flag which prints the line number of each statement in the program as it is executed. The numbers will be displayed within brackets. The Troff (Trace Off) command turns off the Tron command.

Example

```
Ok
100  X = 100
200  FOR I =1 TO 3
300  X = 2 * X
400  PRINT X
500  NEXT
600  END
TRON
Ok
RUN
[100] [200] [300] [400] 200
[500] [300] [400] 400
[500] [300] [400] 800
[500] [600]
Ok
TROFF
Ok
```

USR

■ Cassette
■ Disk
■ Advanced

USR is used to call the machine language subroutine with the argument specified (c).

Configuration

$a = USR[b] (c)$

Where;

b   is the number of the USR routine as given in the Def Usr statement. If b is not included, USR0 will be assumed.

Example

500 A = USR(X/2)

VAL

■ Cassette
■ Disk
■ Advanced

The Val function returns the numeric value of its string argument.

Configuration

$a = VAL(b\$)$

Where;

a   is the numeric value returned by the function.

b$ is the string argument whose numeric value is to be returned.

The Val function eliminates all leading blanks, tabs, and line feeds from the string argument before determining its numeric equivalent.

Example

```
Ok
100  DATA "JOHN WILSON", "212-759-2050"
200  READ NA$, PHONE$
300  A$ = LEFT$ (PHONE$,3)
400  A = VAL(A$)
500  IF A = 212 THEN PRINT NA$ TAB(20) "IS LOCATED IN NY"
600  END
RUN
 JOHN WILSON      IS LOCATED IN NY
Ok
```

VARPTR

■ Cassette
■ Disk
■ Advanced

The Varptr function will return the memory address of the variable specified or the starting memory address of the file control block for the file specified.

Configuration

$$a = VARPTR(variable)$$
$$b = VARPTR(\#filenumber)$$

Where;

a & b is the address returned (0 to 65535). This will be an integer which specifies the offset into the current memory segment. This was defined by the Def Seg statement.

variable may be any type of variable (numeric, array, string).

#filenumber is the filenumber whose file control block starting address is to be returned.

Example

200 FCB = VARPTR(#1)

WAIT

■ Cassette
■ Disk
■ Advanced

The Wait statement is used to halt program execution while examining the status of a machine input port.

Configuration

WAIT port#, a[,b]

Where;

port# is the port number (0 to 65535).

b is an integer constant or expression with which the data read at the port specified is to be XOR'ed.

a is an integer or integer expression which is AND'ed with the value returned by the XOR.

When Wait is executed, the contents of the port address specified is returned. The value returned is XOR'ed with the value given in *b*. If no value is specified for *b*, the default is 0.

The value obtained from the XOR is AND'ed with the value given in *a*. If this value equals 0, WAIT will remain in a loop stopping program execution.

When the result of the WAIT, XOR, and AND operations does not equal 0, program execution will continue with that statement following WAIT.

WHILE, WEND

■ Cassette
■ Disk
■ Advanced

The While statement controls a loop which begins with the While statement and ends with a corresponding WEND statement. The loop will continue to execute as long as the expression named after WHILE evaluates as true (not zero).

Configuration

WHILE *expression*

　:

　:◄——*loop statements*

　:

WEND

If the *expression* following WHILE is true (not zero), the *loop statements* will be executed until WEND is reached. Program control will then branch back to WHILE where it will again check the *expression* to determine whether or not it evaluates as true. If it does, the *loop statements* execute again. If not, program control will branch execution to the statement following WEND.

All WHILE statements must have a corresponding WEND statement. If not, the following error will be displayed:

WEND without WHILE

Example

```
Ok
100  X = 3
200  WHILE X
300  PRINT X
400  X = X – 1
500  WEND
600  END
RUN
 3
 2
 1
Ok
```

WIDTH

■ Cassette
■ Disk
■ Advanced

The Width statement is used to set the output line width.

Configuration

WIDTH *characters*
WIDTH *filenumber, characters*
WIDTH *device, characters*

Where;

characters   indicates the number of characters that WIDTH is to be set to.

filenumber   is the number assigned to a file when it was opened.

device   is a string constant or expression which identifies the device.

When WIDTH is used with a filenumber as per the second configuration example, the width of the device given in the file specification for the file with that filenumber will be set as indicated. This allows the device width to be changed while the file is still open.

Example

100 WIDTH "LPT1:", 80

WRITE

■ Cassette
■ Disk
■ Advanced

The Write statement is used to send data to the screen.

Configuration

WRITE [*expressions*]

Where;

expressions   may be string and/or numeric. These may be delimited by either commas or semi-colons.

The Write statement outputs data much as the Print statement does. One difference between the Write statement and the Print statement, is that when the *expressions* are displayed on the screen with the Write statement, they are separated by commas. Also, with the Write command, strings will be delimited by quotation marks. Also, with the Write statement, blank spaces are not placed in front of positive numbers.

A carriage return/line feed is output after the last item in *expressions* has been output.

Example

```
Ok
100  A$ = "JOHN":B$ = "SMITH":C = 2207
200  WRITE A$, B$, C
RUN
 "JOHN", "SMITH", 2207
Ok
```

WRITE#

■ Cassette
■ Disk
■ Advanced

The Write# statement is used to write data to a sequential file.

Configuration

WRITE# *filenumber, expressions*

Where;

filenumber is the number assigned to the file when it was opened.

expressions can either be string or numeric constants or variables. These will be output to the specified file. The items in *expressions* must be separated with commas or semi-colons.

WRITE# is much like PRINT# except that it delimits strings with quotation marks and inserts commas between the items in *expressions* as they are written. Therefore, specific delimiters need not be included in the list of items output by WRITE#.

A carriage return/line feed character is inserted after the last item in *expressions* has been output.

Example

```
100  WRITE #1, X$, Y$, Z$
```

Appendix A. BASIC Reserved Words

Reserved words are words which have a special meaning in BASIC. They include all BASIC commands, statements, function names, and operator names.

Reserved words are not allowed to be used as variable names in BASIC statements. Also, reserved words must be delimited in BASIC statements so that they can be recognized. Generally, words can be delimited through the use of blank spaces or special characters.

IBM BASIC Reserved Words

ABS	DATE$	HEX$	MKI$	RANDOMIZE	TAB
AND	DEF	IF	MKD$	READ	TAN
ASC	DEFDBL	IMP	MKS$	REM	THEN
ATN	DEFINT	INKEY$	MOD	RENUM	TIME$
AUTO	DEFSNG	INP	MOTOR	RESET	TO
BEEP	DEFSTR	INPUT	NAME	RESTORE	TROFF
BLOAD	DELETE	INPUT#	NEW	RESUME	TRON
BSAVE	DIM	INPUT$	NEXT	RETURN	USING
CALL	DRAW	INSTR	NOT	RIGHT$	USR
CDBL	EDIT	INT	OCT$	RND	VAL
CHAIN	ELSE	KEY	OFF	RSET	VARPTR
CHR$	END	KILL	ON	RUN	WAIT
CINT	EOF	LEFT$	OPEN	SAVE	WEND
CIRCLE	EQV	LEN	OPTION	SCREEN	WHILE
CLEAR	ERASE	LET	OR	SGN	WIDTH
CLOSE	ERL	LINE	OUT	SIN	WRITE
CLS	ERR	LIST	PAINT	SOUND	WRITE#
COLOR	ERROR	LLIST	PEEK	SPACE$	XOR
COM	EXP	LOAD	PEN	SPC	
COMMON	FIELD	LOC	PLAY	SQR	
CONT	FILES	LOCATE	POINT	STEP	
COS	FIX	LOF	POKE	STICK	
CSNG	FNxxxxxx	LOG	POS	STOP	
CSRLIN	FOR	LPOS	PRESET	STR$	
CVD	FRE	LPRINT	PRINT	STRIG	
CVI	GET	LSET	PRINT#	STRING$	
CVS	GOSUB	MERGE	PSET	SWAP	
DATA	GOTO	MID$	PUT	SYSTEM	

Appendix B. IBM Personal Computer Device Names

Device Names

Device Name	Interpretation
KYBD:	**Keyboard**--Used in all versions of BASIC for input.
SCRN:	**Screen**--Used in all versions of BASIC for output.
LPT1:	**First printer**--Used in all versions of BASIC for output.
LPT2:	**Second printer**--Used only in Disk and Advanced versions of BASIC for output.
LPT3:	**Third printer**--Used only in Disk and Advanced versions of BASIC for output.
COM1:	**First asynchronous communications adapter**--Used only in Disk and Advanced BASIC for input and output.
COM2:	**Second asynchronous communications adapter**--Used only in Disk and Advanced BASIC for input and output.
CAS1:	**Cassette tape unit**--Used in all versions of BASIC for input and output.
A:	**First or system disk drive**--Used in Disk and Advanced versions of BASIC for input and output.
B:	**Second disk drive**--Used in Disk and Advanced versions of BASIC for input and output.

Appendix C. IBM BASIC Error Messages

The following give all of the BASIC error messages along with the related error message number and a description of the error.

1 **NEXT without FOR** The variable that follows NEXT does not match with any preceding FOR statement.

2 **Syntax error** The program line contains errors in punctuation or spelling (ex. misspelled reserved word, deleted parentheses, etc.).

3 **RETURN without GOSUB** A RETURN statement is found which does not have a corresponding GOSUB.

4 **Out of data** A READ statement is encountered where no more data items are available to be read from DATA statements.

5 **Illegal function call** A parameter is sent to a system function that is out of range. Examples of the cause of this error include the following:

   - A negative subscript
   - A subscript that is too large.
   - A call to a USR function when the starting address for that function had not been given.
   - A negative record number used with GET or PUT.
   - Trying to list or edit a BASIC program that is protected.
   - An argument for a function or statement that is not legal.

6 **Overflow** A number is larger than that allowed by BASIC. If the overflow occurs with an integer, program execution will stop. With non-integers, machine infinity will be returned with the proper sign.

   If a number is smaller than that allowed by BASIC, an underflow condition will result. A zero will be returned and execution will continue.

7 **Out of Memory** This error occurs when the program is too large for available memory, or if a program contains too many FOR loops or GOSUBS.

8 **Undefined Line Number** A reference is made in the program for a line number that does not exist.

9 **Subscript Out Of Range** An array variable contains a subscript that is outside of the range that was given in the DIM statement.

10 **Duplicate Definition** The same array was defined twice. The following may cause this error:
1. Two DIM statements were included for the same array.
2. A DIM statement is used for an array after a default dimension of 10 had been established previously.
3. An OPTION BASE statement which sets an unacceptable array size is encountered after an array had already been dimensioned by a DIM statement or by default.

11 **Division By Zero** Either division by zero was attempted or an attempt was made to raise to a negative power.

12 **Illegal Direct** An attempt was made to enter a statement in direct mode that can only be entered in indirect.

13 **Type Mismatch** The data used for a variable does not match that variable's type (ex. numeric data for a string variable).

14 **Out Of String Space** BASIC assigns available free memory to string variables until that memory is depleted. When this occurs, this message will be displayed.

15 **String Too Long** The user attempted to create a string in excess of 255 characters.

16 **String Formula Too Complex** The string expression is too long or too complex. Try breaking the expression into smaller, less complex expressions.

17 **Can't Continue** CONT was used in one of the following situations:
- CONT was used to attempt to start a program that had stopped because of an error.
- CONT was used to attempt to start a program that had been changed during a temporary halt in execution.
- CONT was used to attempt to start a program that does not exist.

18 **Undefined User Function** A function was called before it was defined with DEF FN.

19 **NO RESUME** The program branched to an error trapping routine without a RESUME statement.

20 **RESUME Without Error** A RESUME statement is encountered before an error trapping routine was executed.

21 **Unprintable Error** The existing error condition does not have a corresponding error message. This is generally the result of an ERROR statement with an undefined error code.

22 **Missing Operand** No operand following an operator such as +, *, AND.

23 **Line Buffer Overflow** The user tried to enter a line with too many characters.

24 **Device Timeout** Information was not received from an input or output device within an allotted length of time.

25 **Device Fault** A hardware error flag was returned by the interface adapter.

26 **FOR without NEXT** A FOR statement was encountered without a corresponding NEXT.

27 **Out of Paper** Either the printer has run out of paper or it is not turned on.

29 **WHILE without WEND** A WHILE statement was encountered without a corresponding WEND.

30 **WEND without WHILE** A WEND statement was encountered without a corresponding WHILE statement.

50 **FIELD Overflow** the program contains a FIELD statement in which more bytes are allocated for a random file's record length than were specified for that file in its OPEN statement. Another possibility is a situation where the end of the FIELD buffer was reached while a sequential input/output was being performed to a random file (ex. PRINT#, WRITE#, INPUT#, etc.).

51 **Internal Error** Some problem is present internally in BASIC. Call IBM or your IBM dealer with a description of the circumstances under which the error occured.

52 **Bad File Number** A file number is referenced that is not currently assigned to an open file, or is not within the range of valid file numbers specified during initialization. Another possibility is when an invalid device name is used in a file specification or when the filename is invalid.

53 **File Not Found** A file is referenced in a LOAD, KILL, FILES, NAME, or OPEN that does not exist on the diskette on the specified drive.

54 **Bad File Mode** This error occurs when the PUT or GET statement was used with one of the following:
- a sequential file
- a closed file
- to MERGE a non-ASCII file
- to execute an OPEN with a file mode other than input, output, append, or random.

55 **File Already Open** An attempt was made to open a file that had been previously opened for sequential output or an append. This error also occurs when an attempt is made to kill a file that is open.

57 **Device I/O Error** An error occurred during a device I/O operation. Error recovery is not possible in DOS.

58 **File Already Exists** The filename with a NAME statement duplicates that of a filename already being used on that diskette.

61 **Disk Full** The entire diskette space is being used. When this error occurs, all files will be closed.

62 **Input Past End** This error statement indicates that an end of file error occurred. This is caused by an INPUT# statement being executed for a sequential file whose entire data had already been read or for a null file. By using the EOF function, this error can be avoided. Another cause of this error is an attempt to read from a file that had been opened for an append or for output.

63 **Bad Record Number** The record number used in a GET or

PUT statement was either zero or was greater than the allowed maximum (32767).

64 **Bad Filename** An invalid form is used for a filename.

66 **Direct Statement in File** Any ASCII files loaded by LOAD or CHAIN should only contain statements with line numbers. If a direct statement is encountered in a program file being LOAD'ed or CHAIN'ed, the LOAD or CHAIN will be terminated. A common cause of this error is the inclusion of a line feed character.

67 **Device Unavailable** An attempt was made to open a file to a nonexistent device. The device may have been disabled or the hardware may not be present.

69 **Communications Buffer Overflow** A communications input statement was executed with the input buffer already full. When this error condition occurs, use the ON ERROR statement to attempt input again. When ensuing inputs are attempted, the error condition will be cleared unless characters are received at a rate faster than the program can process them. In this case, you can try one of the following:

1. Use /C: option when you start BASIC to increase the size of the communications buffer.
2. Use a hand-shaking routine with the other computer to send a message to tell it to stop sending data so that the receiving computer can empty its buffer.
3. Use a lower baud rate for data transmission and reception.

70 **Disk Write Protect** The user attempted to write to a diskette that was write-protected.

71 **Disk Not Ready** Either a diskette is not in place or the diskette door is open.

72 **Disk Media Error** Generally, this is due to a bad diskette, although the cause can be a hardware related problem. The user should copy any existing data to a new diskette and reformat the bad diskette. If the formatting fails, the diskette is unusable and should be discarded.

73 **Advanced Feature** This error occurs when a program attempts to use an Advanced BASIC feature when Disk BASIC is being used. Load Advanced BASIC and run the program under it.

Appendix D. ASCII Character Codes

In the following table, the ASCII codes will be given with any associated characters and control characters (for codes 0 to 31).

If you wish to display these characters, you can do so by issuing the following statement,

PRINT CHR$(x)

where x is the ASCII code of the character being displayed.

ASCII Value*	Character	Control Character	ASCII Value	Character	Control Character
000	(null)	NUL	016	►	DLE
001	☺	SOH	017	◄	DC1
002	☻	STX	018	↕	DC2
003	♥	ETX	019	‼	DC3
004	♦	EOT	020	¶	DC4
005	♣	ENQ	021	§	NAK
006	♠	ACK	022	▬	SYN
007	(beep)	BEL	023	↨	ETB
008	(backspace)	BS	024	↑	CAN
009	(tab)	HT	025	↓	EM
010	(line feed)	LF	026	→	SUB
011	(home)	VT	027	←	ESC
012	(form feed)	FF	028	(cursor right)	FS
013	(carriage return)	CR	029	(cursor left)	GS
014	♫	SO	030	(cursor right)	RS
015	☼	SI	031	(cursor down)	US

* Decimal

ASCII Value	Character	ASCII Value	Character	ASCII Value	Character
032	(space)	071	G	110	n
033	!	072	H	111	o
034	"	073	I	112	p
035	#	074	J	113	q
036	$	075	K	114	r
037	%	076	L	115	s
038	&	077	M	116	t
039	'	078	N	117	u
040	(	079	O	118	v
041	)	080	P	119	w
042	*	081	Q	120	x
043	+	082	R	121	y
044	,	083	S	122	z
045	–	084	T	123	{
046	.	085	U	124	|
047	/	086	V	125	}
048	0	087	W	126	~
049	1	088	X	127	△
050	2	089	Y	128	Ç
051	3	090	Z	129	ü
052	4	091	[	130	é
053	5	092	\	131	â
054	6	093	]	132	ä
055	7	094	^	133	à
056	8	095	—	134	å
057	9	096	'	135	ç
058	:	097	a	136	ê
059	;	098	b	137	ë
060	<	099	c	138	è
061	=	100	d	139	ï
062	>	101	e	140	î
063	?	102	f	141	ì
064	@	103	g	142	Ä
065	A	104	h	143	Å
066	B	105	i	144	É
067	C	106	j	145	Œ
068	D	107	k	146	Æ
069	E	108	l	147	ô
070	F	109	m	148	ö

ASCII Value	Character	ASCII Value	Character	ASCII Value	Character
149	ò	188	╛	227	π
150	û	189	╜	228	Σ
151	ù	190	╝	229	σ
152	ÿ	191	┐	230	µ
153	Ö	192	└	231	τ
154	Ü	193	┴	232	Φ
155	¢	194	┬	233	Θ
156	£	195	├	234	Ω
157	¥	196	─	235	δ
158	Pt	197	┼	236	∞
159	ƒ	198	╞	237	∅
160	á	199	╟	238	∈
161	í	200	╚	239	∩
162	ó	201	╔	240	≡
163	ú	202	╩	241	±
164	ñ	203	╦	242	≥
165	Ñ	204	╠	243	≤
166	ª	205	═	244	⌠
167	º	206	╬	245	⌡
168	¿	207	╧	246	÷
169	⌐	208	╨	247	≈
170	¬	209	╤	248	°
171	½	210	╥	249	•
172	¼	211	╙	250	·
173	¡	212	╘	251	√
174	«	213	╒	252	ⁿ
175	»	214	╓	253	²
176	░	215	╫	254	■
177	▒	216	╪	255	(blank 'FF')
178	▓	217	┘		
179	│	218	┌		
180	┤	219	█		
181	╡	220	▄		
182	╢	221	▌		
183	╖	222	▐		
184	╕	223	▀		
185	╣	224	α		
186	║	225	β		
187	╗	226	Γ		

Appendix E. Extended Code For Use With INKEY$

Certain keys or key combinations cannot be represented with standard ASCII codes. These are represented with extended codes. The INKEY$ variable can be used to read such a code from the keyboard into a variable.

If a two character string is returned via INKEY$, the first character of that string should be the null character (00 hex). Generally, the second character can be used to allow determination of the key that was pressed. The ASCII codes for the second character are given in decimal in the following table with their associated keys.

Second Code	Meaning
3	(null character) NUL
15	(shift tab) ←
16-25	ALT Q, W, E, R, T, Y, U, I, O, P
30-38	ALT A, S, D, F, G, H, J, K, L
44-50	ALT Z, X, C, V, B, N, M
59-68	Function keys F1 through F10 (when disabled as soft keys).
71	Home
72	Cursor Up
73	Pg Up
75	Cursor Left
77	Cursor Right
79	End
80	Cursor Down
81	Pg Down
82	Ins
83	Del
84-93	F11 through F20 (Uppercase F1 through F10)
94-103	F21 through F30 (CTRL F1 through F10)
104-113	F31 through F40 (ALT F1 through F10)
114	CTRL Prtsc
115	CTRL Cursor Left (Previous Word)
116	CTRL Cursor Right (Next Word)
117	CTRL End
118	CTRL Pg Dn
119	CTRL Home
120-131	ALT 1, 2, 3, 4, 5, 6, 7, 8, 9, 0, -, =
132	CTRL Pg Up

INDEX

A: 294
ABS 110, 111, 158
Address 20
Advanced BASIC 24, 64
All Points Addressable Mode 45, 47
Alphanumeric Mode 45, 46
Alt Key 147
ALU 20
AND Operator 117, 118, 260
APPEND 127, 145, 238
Arithmetic Expression 73
Arithmetic Operators 72
Arrays 87, 88
ASC 106, 107, 158
ASCII Codes 300, 301, 302
Asynchronous Communications
  Adapter 47, 48
ATN 109, 159
Attribute Code 43
AUTO 159, 160

B: 294
BASIC, Advanced 24
BASIC, Cassette 24
BASIC, Command entry 61
BASIC, Disk 24
BASIC Intrepreter 14, 24
BASIC, Start-Up Display 60
BEEP 161
Bit 20
BLOAD 161, 162
BLOS 14, 16, 18
Boolean Operators 117
Bootstrap Loader 14, 15
Box Filled Parameter 116
Box Parameter 116
Branching Statements 83, 84
BSAVE 163

Bugs 154
Byte 20

CALL 163, 164
CAS1: 294
Cassette BASIC 24, 63
CDBL 110, 111, 164
CHAIN 165
CHR$ 106, 107, 166
CINT 110, 111, 167
CIRCLE 167
CLEAR 168
CLOSE 129, 169
CLS 169
COLOR 114, 115, 170, 171, 172, 173
Color Graphics Monitor Adapter
  45, 47
COM 173, 174
COM1: 294
COM2: 294
COM OFF 232
COM STOP 232
Command Mode 64, 65
COMMON 174
Compiled Language 37
Compiler 37
Concatenation 101, 102
Conditional Statements 83
Constants 67
CONT 174, 175
Control Key Combinations 55
Copy 143
COS 108, 175
COT 108
CP/M-86 33, 34, 35
CPS-80 Printer 39, 40, 41
CPU 20
Crosstalk 43

CSC 108
CSNG 110, 111, 175, 176
CSRLIN 176
Current Drive 143
CVD 176
CVI 176
CVS 176

Data Files 123
DATA Statement 90, 91, 92, 177
DATE$ 177, 178
Debugging 154
Default Drive 143
DEFDBL 180, 181
DEF FN 112, 179, 180
DEFINT 180, 181
DEF SEG 181
DEFSNG 180, 181
DEFSTR 180, 181
DEF USR 182
DELETE 148, 166, 182, 183
Delimiter 124
Device Name 125
DIM Statement 88, 89, 183
DIR 142
Disk BASIC 24, 63
DISKCOMP 140, 141
DISKCOPY 138, 139, 140
Disk Drives 25
Diskettes, double sided 32
Diskettes, single sided 32
Diskette Write Protection 32, 33
Disk Drives 25
Disk Operating Systems 33
Disks, floppy 26, 28, 29, 134, 135
Disks, hard 26, 27
Disks, Winchester 26, 27, 28
DOS 25, 136
DOS, Keyboard Usage 55, 56
DOS, Start-Up 59, 60, 61
DOS, Start-Up Display 60
Double Precision Data 69, 70
DRAW 183, 184, 185
Dynamic RAM 14

EDIT 185
Editor 148
END 186
EOF 132, 186, 187

EQ 102
EQV Operator 117, 119
ERASE 142, 187, 188
ERL 188
ERR 188
ERROR 154, 189, 190
Error Message 295
Execute Mode 64, 65
EXP 110, 190
Exponentiation 73, 75
Extended Codes 303

FIELD 123, 190, 191
FILE 123, 191
Filename 125
Filename Extension 125
File Specification 125
Firmware 14
FIX 110, 111, 192
Floating Point Division 75
Floppy Disks 26, 28, 29
FORMAT 137
Format String 96, 97, 98, 99
Formatting Characters 96, 97, 98, 99
FOR NEXT 193, 194
FRE 195
Functions, User-Defined 112

GE 102
GET 196, 197
GOSUB 93, 94, 198
GOTO 84, 85, 199
Graphics 112, 113, 114, 115, 116
GT 102

Hard Disks 26, 27
Hard Sectoring 30, 31
Head 26
HEX$ 199, 200
High Resolution Graphics 47, 112, 113

IF, THEN 83, 200, 201
IMP Operator 117, 119
Index Hole 30
Index Variable 82
INKEY$ 201, 303
INP 202
INPUT 80, 81, 126, 202, 203
INPUT# 133, 204, 205

INPUT$ 205, 206
INSTR 206, 207
INT 110, 111, 207
Integer Data 69
Integer Division 75
Intel 8087 22, 23
Intel 8088 9, 21, 22
Interpreted Language 37
Interrupt Vectors 18, 19

KEY 208, 209, 210
Keyboard 48, 49, 50
Keyboard, Numeric Keys 52, 53
Keyboard, Program Control Keys 49
Keyboard, Program Function Keys 50, 51
Keyboard Unit 9, 10
KEY OFF 235
KEY ON 235
KEY STOP 236
Keyword 71
KILL 210
KYBD: 294

LE 102
LEFT$ 103, 211
LEN 103, 211
LET 212
Line Editor 148
LINE INPUT 214
LINE INPUT# 215
LIST 216, 217
LLIST 217, 218
Line Numbers 64, 147
LINE Statement 115, 116, 212, 213
LOAD 130, 131, 144, 218, 219
LOC 219, 220
LOCATE 220, 221
LOF 221, 222
LOG 110, 222
Logic Errors 154
Logical Operators 117
Loops 81, 82
Low Resolution 47
LPOS 223
LPRINT 223, 224
LPRINT Statement 79, 95
LPRINT USING 224
LPT1: 294

LPT2: 294
LPT3: 294
LSET 225
LT 102

MATCH 103
Matrix Printer 10
Medium Resolution 47
Medium Resolution Graphics 112, 113, 114
Megabyte 16
MERGE 165, 226, 227
MID$ 103, 104, 105, 106, 227
MKD$ 228, 229
MKI$ 228, 229
MKS$ 228, 229
Modulo Arithmetic 75
Monochrome Display 10, 38, 39
Monochrome Display/Printer Adapter Card 42, 44
MOTOR 229
Multiplication 75

NAME 230
NE 102
Negation 75
NEW 148, 230, 231
NOT Operator 117, 118

OCT$ 231
ON COM 231, 232, 233
ON ERROR 233, 234
ON GOSUB 234, 235
ON GOTO 234, 235
ON KEY 235, 236
ON PEN 236, 237
ON STRIG 237, 238
OPEN 126, 127, 128, 144, 238
OPEN COM 240, 242
OPTION BASE 242
OR Operator 117, 118, 260
Order of Evaluation 74, 122
OUT 242, 243
OUTPUT 126, 145, 238, 239, 240

PAINT 243, 244
Palette 115
Parity Checks 16
Parallel Communications 41, 42

Parameter 71
PC DOS 33, 34
p-CODE 36
PEEK 244
PEN 245, 246
PEN OFF 236, 237, 245, 246
PEN ON 236, 237, 245, 246
PEN STOP 237, 245, 246
Pixel 114
PLAY 246, 247, 248
p-Machine Emulator 36
POINT 248, 249
POKE 249
POS 250
PRESET 115, 257, 258, 259
PRINT Statement 79, 95, 250, 251
PRINT USING 251, 252, 253, 254, 255
PRINT# 255, 256, 257
PRINT# USING 255
Printer Cable 42, 43
Printer Operation 57, 58
Program 63
Program Entry 65, 66, 67
Program Files 123
Program Line 147
PSET 115, 257, 258, 259
PUT 258, 259, 260

RAM 9, 10, 14, 15, 17
Random Access 26
Random Files 129
Random Number Generator 100
RANDOMIZE 101, 261
READ Statement 100, 268
Records 123
Relational Operators 76
REM 262, 263
Remark Statement 78
RENAME 142
RENUM 263, 264
Reserved Word 71, 293
RESTORE Statement 91, 264, 265
RESUME 265, 266
RETURN 93, 94, 198, 266, 267
RF Modulator 47
RIGHT$ 103, 104, 267, 268
RND Statement 100, 268
ROM 9, 14, 15
RSET 255, 264

RUN 269
Run-Time Monitor 37

SAVE 130, 144, 148, 270
SCRN: 294
SCREEN 113, 271, 272, 273
SEC 108
Sectors 25, 27
Seed 100
Sequential Access 26
Sequential Files 129
Serial Communications 41, 42
SGN 110, 111, 273
SIN 108, 273, 274
Single Precision Data 69, 70
Single Sided Diskettes 32
Soft Sectoring 30, 31
SOUND 274
SPC 275, 276
SPACE$ 275
SQR 110, 276
STR$ 106, 107, 278
Start-Up Procedure 59, 60, 61
Static RAM 14
Status Line 44
STEP Statement 116
STICK 276, 277
STOP 277, 278
STRIG 279, 280
STRIG OFF 237, 279, 280
STRIG ON 237, 279, 280
STRIG STOP 238, 279, 280
STRING 280, 281
String Handling 101
Subroutines 93
Subscripted Variables 87, 88
Subscripts 87
SWAP 281
SYSTEM 141, 282
System Board 12, 13
System Level 141
System Unit 9, 10

TAB Statement 96, 282
Tables 87, 88
TAN 108, 283
Text Mode 112, 113
TIME$ 283, 284
Trace Flag 155

Tracks 29
TROFF 154, 155, 284, 285
TRON 154, 155, 284, 285
Truncated 147
Truncation 69
TYPE 142

UCSD p-System 33, 35
User-Defined Functions 112
USR 285, 286

VAL 106, 107, 286
Variable Names 68, 69
Variables 67, 68
VARPTR 287

WAIT 287, 288
WEND 288, 289
WHILE 288, 289
WIDTH Statement 99, 100, 289
Winchester Disks 26, 27, 28
WRITE 290, 291
WRITE# 131, 132, 291
Write Protection Diskettes 32, 33, 134

XOR Operator 117, 119, 260, 261